FED UP

WOMEN AND FOOD IN AMERICA

CATHERINE MANTON

BERGIN & GARVEY

Westport, Connecticut • London

Library of Congress Cataloging-in-Publication Data

Manton, Catherine, 1942–
    Fed up : women and food in America / Catherine Manton.
      p. cm.
    Includes bibliographical references and index.
    ISBN 0–89789–448–0 (alk. paper).—ISBN 0–89789–629–7 (pbk. :
alk. paper)
    1. Women—United States—Social conditions. 2. Women—United
States—Psychology. 3. Food—Social aspects—United States.
4. Food habits—United States. I. Title.
HQ1410.M355   1999
305.4'0973—dc21   98–19215

British Library Cataloguing in Publication Data is available.

Library of Congress Catalog Card Number: 98–19215
ISBN: 0–89789–448–0
     0–89789–629–7 (pbk.)

First published in 1999

Bergin & Garvey, 88 Post Road West, Westport, CT 06881
An imprint of Greenwood Publishing Group, Inc.

Printed in the United States of America

The paper used in this book complies with the
Permanent Paper Standard issued by the National
Information Standards Organization (Z39.48–1984).

Copyright Acknowledgments

The author and publisher gratefully acknowledge permission to use the following material:

From *Appetite for Change* by Warren J. Belasco. Copyright © 1989 by Warren J. Belasco.
Reprinted by permission of Pantheon Books, a division of Random House, Inc.

From *Revolution at the Table: The Transformation of the American Diet* by Harvey A. Levenstein.
Copyright © 1988 by Harvey A. Levenstein. Used by permission of Oxford University Press,
Inc.

Excerpt from *Perfection Salad: Women and Cooking at the Turn of the Century* by Laura Shapiro.
Copyright © 1986 by Laura Shapiro. Reprinted by permission of North Point Press, a
division of Farrar, Straus & Giroux, Inc.

Excerpt from *Perfection Salad: Women and Cooking at the Turn of the Century* by Laura Shapiro. Reprinted by permission of International Creative Management, Inc. Copyright © 1986 by Laura
Shapiro.

Every reasonable effort has been made to trace the owners of copyright materials in this book,
but in some instances this has proven impossible. The author and publisher will be glad to receive information leading to more complete acknowledgments in subsequent printings of the
book and in the meantime extend their apologies for any omissions.

Contents

Preface

I have always been passionately involved with food in one way or another.

As a child my relationship with food was adversarial in many ways. Being diagnosed with 53 food allergies as a toddler meant that most of the foods other family members ate were off limits for me. My extremely limited diet did, however, provide me a special status in relation to my older sisters. I was the "sickly" one who got lots of attention and fuss from my parents, especially my mother.

My mother, Elva, was an accomplished cook in the best tradition of domestic science. Her children had a balanced diet and ate what she put on their plates, regardless of personal food preferences. Meal times were serious business, and snacking between meals was not allowed. Elva made it quite clear that she did not welcome any help in the kitchen, saying there was only room for one person to cook in that space. Given the family's food arrangement, it was not suprising that I ate only out of duty throughout my childhood.

With marriage and a subsequent move from my parents' home, I was forced to learn something about cooking. This "wifely duty" quickly captured my interest as I joined other women of my generation in a progression from soup-based recipes (1950s), through French cuisine (1960s), to health food (1970s) over the next few decades.

During the 1980s I gradually became aware of the different ways food had become an organizing principle in my life. The old kitchen in my Boston townhouse always had been the heart of the building.

My daughter and I spent our time together in that place. Friends always seemed to end up crowded into that narrow long room, regardless of the availability of other larger rooms for socializing. I began reading books *about* food in addition to the cookbooks I had been collecting for decades. I came to realize that cooking centered me when the rest of life left me confused or distracted. Preparing and eating food provided many of my happiest moments each day.

My intellectual exploration of the meaning of food for women eventually affected my academic life. In 1988 I developed and began teaching a course, "Food in Women's Lives," in our Women's Studies program at the University of Massachusetts at Boston. Within a few years I realized a more accurate title for the course would be "Food and Feminism," as an analysis of women's relationship with food from this perspective now seemed necessary to fully understand the continuum of complicated experiences women have with this life necessity. However, what I originally construed to be a positive, nurturing relationship was only part of the picture; an overwhelming number of students whose writing documented troubled, even pathological, relationships with food mandated a modification of my original approach in thinking about food. Furthermore, my educational background and academic tenure encouraged a feminist analysis of women's intense ambivalence about food and body image at the century's end.

During those early years of the 1990s, I also had begun practicing clinical psychology, and encountered many clients with all kinds of eating disturbances. My academic investigation of food suggested some radical changes in my treatment of these clients; feminist therapy in conjunction with nutritional and cooking instruction seemed a logical course of action. Thus Appetite for Change was begun on an experimental basis to test my working hypothesis that women with eating disturbances really can heal themselves.

One final shift in emphasis has occurred in my life during these last years of the twentieth century. A personal awareness of the relationship of individual behavior to planetary health has grown from my study of ecofeminism and has motivated me to go "back to basics" in my personal life, to pare down my lifestyle and focus on the hard kernels of existence that really are most worthy of my attention and effort.

It has taken four years to write this book, which now exists as one worthwhile kernel of my existence.

Acknowledgments

I would never have begun this writing project if my (later) agent, John Harney, had not suggested it to me originally, and then kept after me for five years until it was done. On the home front, my daughter, Mindy Sobota, provided the calm, clear-eyed vision of one who knew I could do it. When the initial idea of a contributed volume faded, my colleague and good friend, Elaine Morse, stepped forth in fine form to produce material I myself could not write. Ten years of students in my "Food and Feminism" classes at the University of Massachusetts at Boston have yielded endless, insightful material on women's very complicated relationship with food.

Thanks to my colleagues in Women's Studies for originally supporting my proposal for such a "radical" course as "Food and Feminism" in the days when food was *not* considered a subject worthy of serious academic pursuit. As I pushed to finish the book this past year, Jean, Ann, and Elaine created a work environment for me requiring few additional academic responsibilities within our program; that extra time was such a luxury!

Warren Belasco, Laura Shapiro, and Harvey Levenstein all neatly side-stepped writing chapters for me but, more important, gave me the confidence to do the writing myself. In particular, Warren and Laura both provided warm words of encouragement during the two summers I hunkered down in chilly Maine, distilling their wisdom into my own words. Margaret Cope was a breath of summer the second year with her insistence that I present my views at a University of Massachusetts Medical Center forum the following year.

Sometimes small gestures trigger great gains. In this manner, Charlotte Fritz, Michelle McPhee, and Colin Stewart all provided fertile ground for indispensable material in what you are about to read.

Chapter 1

Food Is Everyone's First Language

Anthropologists agree with Paul Kwan[1] that food is a central expressive element in any culture. What and how we eat, and with whom, reveals much about our desires and relationships. A basic assumption underlying this volume is that women traditionally have used food as a means of nurturing and caring for others.

HOW IT ALL BEGAN

Different social sex roles evolved from the contributions each sex made to the group's food supply. In the earliest known examples of human culture, a sexual division of labor encouraged females as primary providers, preparers, and processors of food within the family unit.[2] The raw foods females gathered were not incidental to the group's diet; to the contrary, the vast majority of the group's nutritional needs were met by female contributions to the food supply *after* men evolved into big-game hunters.[3] Females also were responsible for food storage so that the group could survive lean times when fresh foods were not readily available. Over time, females took an additional role—as healers, using foodstuffs and other plant matter in the care of the sick and injured. All of these important roles gave females a strong sense of worthiness and value within the family and the wider social group.

DISRUPTIONS IN TRADITIONAL ROLE

The relationship between the sexes in the cooperative division of labor surrounding food was not altered radically until patriarchy flourished within agrarian societies. Women had much less personal power and social status under this new social arrangement since ownership of land (and people) now resided exclusively in the hands of individual males. Agrarian labor required considerable physical strength and the need to work far from home, both requirements that most women found difficult to fulfill. Because women now worked rather exclusively within the husband's home at a distance from their own kin, they also lost any opportunity to create influencial roles for themselves within the larger community. Not only were the sexes now isolated from each other, but women also were isolated from one another and from public life.

A riddle: What do a tin can, a test tube, a recipe file box,
    and a baby bottle all have in common?
Answer: The industrial revolution.

More than one hundred years ago, the industrial revolution created a new technology that made canned or processed food available to ordinary folks on a large scale. The only obstacle to manufacturers' profits was the need to motivate women to buy this new kind of food. Women had to be convinced that processed food was healthier for their families while also saving food preparation time. What resulted was an extremely successful advertising campaign to convince housewives that processed food was superior to any food they previously had made "from scratch." Capitalists who owned food processing factories were quite successful in selling their products. However, the advertising that sold products also caused women to question their adequacy as homemakers; it also alienated them from the sensual, nurturing pleasures involved in food preparation.

Another successful advertising campaign, this time the brain child of the newest specialty within the American Medical Association, convinced mothers to shift from breast to bottle feeding. Pediatricians' seemingly modern idea was based on the intentionally destructive premise that women's bodies were inadequate, even when performing the biological function of the mammary glands.

Domestic scientists, with their white lab coats and confident use of fact, further undermined women's previous knowledge of how best to feed their families. Immigrants and working-class women especially were targeted for dietary change by food reformers; as a result, previous culinary traditions were abandoned by these groups.

Women increasingly worked outside the home and needed quick, easily prepared food that nourished, perhaps more than it nurtured, their families. The creation of the make-believe perfect housewife, Betty Crocker, encouraged a lasting change in the way American housewives cooked with the introduction of written recipes for the first time on a widespread basis. No longer was it necessary, or even acceptable, for an American housewife to create meals by adding a "little of this to a little of that," using whatever she happened to have in her kitchen or garden. Advertising campaigns such as this wildly successful one by General Mills caused many women to question their previously intuitive, spontaneous approach to food.

By the early decades of the twentieth century, women could even be food professionals, but a career in the new educational field of home economics demanded scientific rigor in the kitchen while denying any of the sensual pleasures cooks formerly could anticipate in the preparation and consumption of their culinary achievements.

Middle-class women increasingly fulfilled roles other than those of mother and homemaker as the twentieth century progressed. Full partnership in a modern marriage required women to remain sexually alluring to their husbands while, at the same time, to develop social skills that furthered their husbands' careers. These new roles concomitantly imposed new restrictions on the acceptable size of a woman's body.

Consideration of all these phenomena spawned by the industrial revolution at the turn of the twentieth century clarifies the historic cultural, social, economic, and political forces that have contributed to contemporary American women's estrangement from food.[4]

TAKING UP TOO MUCH SPACE

It certainly was no coincidence that twice during the twentieth century American women gained some measure of personal and political power at precisely the same time society demanded them to have smaller bodies.

Weight expectations shifted downwards—from the image of Lillian Russell in the 1890s to the flappers of the 1920s—and involved about twice the number of pounds as years. Increasingly adversarial attitudes toward food consumption and its impact on body size materialized as America approached mid-century, and the dieting industry was born in the 1950s. The popularity of dieting programs increased social pressure on women to either become smaller or experience shame and guilt over their perceived failure to achieve the body shape advertising and modern media dictated to them. In that same decade even our sex goddess, Marilyn Monroe, wore a size 12–14 dress, but by the 1960s Twiggy had shrunken desirable body size to that of a preadolescent boy.

Feminists have observed that the two major cultural demands for a significantly smaller body size occurred in America at exactly the same time women themselves were demanding greater economic and political rights. The trim and muscular flapper was the ideal body type of the 1920s when real women finally were successful in getting the vote and other women's rights. In the 1960s we got both the anorexic Twiggy and the second wave of feminism. Both decades involved a cultural backlash making one demand: that women must have smaller bodies in response to women actually demanding and occupying more cultural space.

The supposed epidemic of eating disorders erupting in the United States during the latter part of the twentieth century has not been accidental. The roots of modern women's war with food were planted in the industrial revolution; an emphasis on new economic markets at the expense of individual food production resulted in changed expectations for Americans' eating patterns. Incipient eating disturbances also were nurtured by social attitudes suggesting that women no longer were capable of feeding themselves or their families. Low levels of self-esteem and self-confidence inevitably grew from this schism in the traditional role.

American women have grown increasingly alienated from their traditional social sex role in the late twentieth century, especially as a result of their loss of personal responsibility and pride in the procurement and preparation of their families' food. Many clinicians and social scientists have noted the corresponding increase in eating disorders related to that loss. Being actively involved with the food eaten and prepared for others offers a wonderful opportunity to both give and receive nurturance through the medium of food.

Anorexia, bulimia, and compulsive eating became much more common as women were disconnected from these positive elements of food, and food was viewed as the enemy. Obviously this rupture in the traditional role has created a condition of dis-ease for many modern American women.

FOOD AS METAPHOR

A feminist analysis of eating disorders as a reaction to patriarchal oppression is valid; it is important to emphasize the ways women's relationship with food has been manipulated by capitalism, the food industry in particular, over the last 150 years. The incidence of eating disorders has increased in direct proportion to the expansion of food processing and the mass-marketing of food in America. Domestic science has unwittingly served as the academic arm of capitalism; in addition, food reformers have actively discouraged any personally rewarding relationship with food. Most feminist analysis, however, has focused exclusively on the social, economic, and political aspects of this oppression to explain eating disturbances. This sort of analysis has emphasized external influences; the private, inner life of a woman usually has been ignored, even though psychology long ago demonstrated the importance of subjective, emotional forces in determining human behavior.

It is important, therefore, to keep women's basic, passionate relationship with food in perspective. Food is a metaphor for most women's emotional lives. Food is a barometer for women's feelings about themselves and the world. Food can represent the conflicts a woman experiences in her life, serving as a battleground for her struggles to control the forces she perceives to be dictating her life. In a more positive way, food can symbolize the nurturance and love a woman feels toward others. Food can be a vehicle for the expression of one's sensuous nature. When a woman feels good about herself, she usually considers herself in control of her eating, and she is able to appreciate the sensual, pleasurable qualities of food.

The last 150 years, however, has seen an increase in American women's negative, as opposed to neutral or positive, feelings about themselves in relation to food. Negative feelings have ranged from merely questioning one's ability to provide healthy, satisfying food for self and loved ones, to severely self-critical indictments that often result from internalized cultural demands for women to achieve impossible standards in mind and body. Regardless of the degree of severity, such negativity always reflects an ambivalence about food pervasive in American culture. Since eating is necessary for survival, consistently negative feelings about food provide a fertile breeding ground for eating disorders.

DENIAL OF DESIRE

One hundred years ago it already was believed that one should not eat just what one enjoys. Apparently even then most people believed that the body could not be trusted to accurately judge what foods were needed for optimal health.

Domestic science assumed that middle-class women, just like their upper-class role models, preferred not to deal directly with food because it was too "dirty" or "mundane" to warrant their attention. A shortage of servants, however, coincided with the rise of the middle class in America, and genteel women increasingly were forced to be directly responsible for the preparation of their family's food. So these housewives went to cooking school to learn how to manage meals and other household duties in a modern, scientific way. It is significant that, even after expending great effort to make pretty, time-consuming dishes in domestic science school kitchens, female students were not allowed to even sample their own culinary accomplishments. Experiencing pleasure in the sensual aspects of cooking and eating was never acknowledged, much less encouraged, in this sterile environment.

With their broader perspective on eating behavior, culinary historians have observed that modern fast food and brand name products appear to satisfy a basic need for the familiar and the comfortable in an individual's food choices. The popularity of so-called comfort food and the high level of bingeing, both evident in 1990s America, have provided strong evidence that this basic need might be even stronger now than in the past.

Women generally are expected to nurture others with little regard for their own needs for nurturance. To some degree, all women with eating disorders are unable to nurture themselves in ways that do not involve food or eating. A compulsive eater, for example, is stereotyped as a nurturer who knows no boundaries. An anorexic woman cannot be nourished. A bulimic woman cannot sustain the nurturing process; her purges renounce the preceding satisfaction of that need. A woman need not be labeled with one of these three major eating disorders, however, to feel trapped in a double-bind: whether to nurture self or others.

To end discussion of women's personal relationships with food at this point would deny women an opportunity to heal themselves of discomforting relationships with food and the world around them; it also would discourage women's collective refusal to accept an environment that encourages them to hurt and even destroy themselves in an ongoing struggle with food and body image. Together women must re-establish a more positive, constructive relationship with both food and their bodies, and an environment that makes positive constructive living possible.

WHAT'S WRONG WITH AMERICAN FOOD

Two major criticisms of the American diet, first articulated in the 1960s but continuing today, are that the cuisine is not sophisticated enough and, at the same time, the food is not healthy enough. The former viewpoint resulted in the enormous popularity of Julia Child during the last four decades of the century. A secondary result of the 1960s love affair with French food was a growing appreciation of food as a means of self-definition. But the fusion of food with identity has also caused considerable self-consciousness, perhaps even anxiety and guilt, about what is eaten.

During the last two decades of the twentieth century, tremendous affluence has existed for certain segments of the American population. But escalating property values have prevented many younger adults from the home ownership their parents' generation took for granted. For some working adults of the 1980s and 1990s, lifestyle choices, including conspicuous food consumption, have replaced the more enduring assets older generations worked to acquire. For these Americans, social class is defined in materialistic terms; from this perspective, the cost of food, both eaten at home and out, can never be too great if it guarantees membership in a particular social class.

Prior to the excesses of the 1980s, self-consciousness about food consumption usually occurred only in dieting centers. Now it is occurring for Americans in general. The previously vast realm of guilt-provoking areas in life has shrunk to a "beleaguered enclave" dominated by a morally problematic interaction with food: "At the heart of this new food guilt is a migration of both our eroticism and our moral focus from our groins to our guts" (Iggers, 1993, p. 58). It seems that, for some Americans, the determinants of personal identity have shifted from one's attachments to the social world, typical of Victorian times when sex was loaded with expectation and responsibility, to a more transient world where autonomy and privacy dominate and individuals define themselves by what they consume rather than by connections.

Fat phobia, which refers to an inappropriate psychological fear or anxiety about dietary or body fat, first appeared in the 1960s when Americans became obsessed with the relationship of dietary fat to coronary disease and cholesterol. It has been an easy mental shift to consider fat on the body and in the blood vessels as a reflection of the amount of fat in our diets. Medical admonishments of a diet heavy in fat and a fat body from lack of proper exercise have dovetailed with a concomitant movement back to natural (meaning less environmentally contaminated) food. Organic natural foods have been considered the logical solution to both concerns, at least for the "back to nature" segment of the American population. Eating naturally also can be felt to improve one's spiritual and mental state. All three benefits have suggested that organic natural food is superior to any other food available in this country, an opinion held by an increasing number of Americans. Another food status symbol had been born, therefore, since everyone already knew "we are what we eat." By logical extension, individuals who eat only organic natural food acquire the moral superiority already attributed to that category of food.

Near the end of the twentieth century, marketing researchers for a major national newspaper have reported that the American public never before reached consensus so quickly or completely as it did on the diet necessary for good health. Fat has become the universal villain; concern about dietary fat has transcended all class, race, and regional barriers. So beliefs that until the 1990s were considered primarily a "women's thing," perhaps a "white women's thing," now have permeated the entire American culture: an ongoing obsession with dietary and body fat.

The paradox, of course, is that the number of people in the population who are overweight has increased in direct proportion to America's growing preoccupation with fat. The conflict involved in competing desires for a slim, healthy body and familiar, comfortable high-fat foods has been cast as "a struggle between good and evil, between the baseness of human instinct and the glory of rational restraint" since "we're a country with a lively appreciation of sin, and our eating behavior appears to be colored by it" (O'Neill, 1996a, p. 38). By the end of the century, Americans' food choices certainly had become a nationally broadcasted morality play.

Perhaps simply eating right, watching one's weight, and exercising regularly are no longer enough. Americans at the turn of the century seem to be in a moral search for "wellness," a kind of superstate of mental and physical well-being wherein profound psychological and emotional transformations can be achieved. Behind the motivation for wellness is the belief that perfect adherence to diet and body maintenance, certainly a superior state of moral purity, can deter the aging process itself.

KITCHEN-COUNTER REFORMS

If "the personal is political," as in this volume's use of the phrase to encourage understanding of the relationship between eating disturbances and cultural forces promoting thinness, then I would suggest that the reverse also must be true: "The political is personal," meaning that individuals can manifest some control over food sources in their efforts to improve the health of their own food supply and that of the planet by alterations in diet.

Each American can choose to make "kitchen-counter reforms," a phrase used in Washington, D.C. to describe dietary changes that can influence policy governing the production and provision of food in America. Each citizen individually can choose to "vote with your fork"[5] each time she or he goes food shopping or eats out. Reform is accomplished by following four simple culinary rules: eat indigenous, organic, fresh, and seasonal food. It also helps to reduce meat consumption since growing feed for animals raised for slaughter is an inefficient use of valuable farm land. Adherence to these rules discourages developing countries from forcing peasants to grow cash crops on land badly needed for subsistence farming. Energy resources are not wasted flying out-of-season foods long distances for consumption by individuals willing to pay any price so that they can eat what they want when they want it. Following the rules also provides community and financial support for local farmers struggling to maintain their small, independent farms. Eating organically reduces the use of fertilizers, pesticides, antibiotics, steroids, and other chemicals and drugs that both pollute our food supply and our environment. Perhaps this strategy is most attractive because the individual food consumer can actively do something to help resolve huge, global issues such as world hunger, global environmental pollution, and food supply contamination. In the past, the feminist movement taught us that an oppressed individual will not feel nearly so powerless if there is some action she can take on her own. Since Americans eat several times a day, there is endless potential for reaffirming our personal beliefs about ideal food consumption if we follow the culinary rules generated by kitchen-counter reforms.

Chapter 2

Woman the Provider
Elaine S. Morse

Throughout human history, growing or buying, processing, storing, and cooking largely have been female activities. In addition to being the sex primarily responsible for these food activities, women traditionally have expressed love and nurturance through this work. Why is this so? Has it always been this way? Why is this an important field of inquiry? Chapter 2 provides answers to these questions. One assumption underlying this chapter is that food is extremely important in understanding social behavior and culture. Anthropologists have often stated that those who know what members of a society eat already know a lot about that society. Knowledge of how food is obtained and who prepares it adds considerably to the anthropologist's store of information about the way that society functions (Farb and Armelagos, 1980). Another assumption underlying this chapter is the importance of understanding how change in the division of labor that evolved through the various forms human societies have taken provides insight regarding the disruptions in women's eating and food relationships that manifested in twentieth-century America.

ALL ANIMALS FEED, BUT ONLY HUMANS EAT

Differences in food procurement and eating behavior distinguish human from nonhuman primate societies. In fact the human quest for food was so dramatically different from all other primates that changes in diet and food procurement must have been important factors in the evolutionary changes leading to modern humans. Although the exact details of this evolutionary process cannot be known, a surprising number of facts and statements about who was eating what, where, when, and how can be inferred from fossils and archaeological materials, from studies of our living primate relatives among monkeys and apes, and from ethnographic studies of living and historic hunting and gathering people.

Humans, chimpanzees, and gorillas apparently diverged from a common ancestor as recently as 5 or 6 million years ago. Fossil discoveries provide evidence that the earliest hominids lived on the African savannas around 3.5 million years ago. About the size of small chimpanzees and with somewhat larger brains, they walked upright and began making stone tools at least two million years ago. Between 300,000 and 100,000 years ago hominids with human-size brains were evolving in many parts of Europe, Asia, and Africa; about 50,000 years ago these protohominid ancestors had evolved into an essentially modern Homo sapiens. Assuming that protohominid ancestors evolved from a baseline of characteristics shared by living non-human primates, some of the ways in which humans are similar to non-human primates can be enumerated. The commonly shared necessities to feed or locomote in an arborial habitat require a small number of offspring per birth; prolongation of gestation and infancy; complexity of social behavior, arising from the prolonged mother-infant relationship and intense care given to each offspring; and enlargement of the brain (Slocum, 1975; Zihlman, 1981).

While humans share many features with non-human primates, differences between the behavior of humans' closest relatives, the chimpanzees, and even the simplest hunter-gatherers are enormous. The most striking difference between hominids and apes relate to the development of bipedalism in hominids. Additional human traits include a longer gestation period and long period of infant dependency; absence of body hair; year-round sexual receptivity of females replacing the estrous cycle; and a larger and complex brain enabling the development of language, complex tool-making, and other cultural adaptations. Human practices included regular use of tools to obtain food; carrying food back to a home base or camp; and sharing according to established rules.

None of these behaviors have been found among chimpanzees or any other non-human primate (Slocum, 1975).

Unfortunately fossil records cannot reveal when these practices began or how they developed; disagreements, differing interpretations, and conflicting views have resulted among anthropologists.

FORAGING SOCIETIES[1]

One popular reconstruction of early human behavior is captured in the phrase, "man the hunter." In this hypothesis, meat-eating signaled man's separation from the apes. Male hunters provided the meat, presumed to be the main item in early hominid diets, and invented tools and weapons for hunting. Thus the male played the main economic role, protecting and supporting "his" dependent females and young.

Feminist anthropologists have criticized the "man the hunter" model, exposing the underlying male bias. Slocum (1975) has observed that "while this reconstruction is certainly ingenious, it gives one the decided impression that only half the species—the male half—did any evolving" (p. 42). Such reconstruction might best be explained by an obsession with hunting that prevented predominantly male anthropologists from taking an objective look at women's probable role in shaping the human adaptation (Zihlman, 1981).

What Actually Was Eaten

Despite the persistence of the "man the hunter" hypothesis, today it generally is believed that early hominids relied on plants much more than animal foods for their sustenance. The distinctive features of the hominid arrangement of teeth, for example, suggest a demanding vegetarian diet that required a lot of milling and grinding (Gordon, 1987). Furthermore, modern hunter-gatherers by far obtain the major part of their diet by collecting roots, fibers, seeds, fruits, nuts, grubs, insects, and the like. The meat produced by hunting, except for northernmost hunters, constitutes only 20 to 30 percent of these people's total diet. Wild game from the hunt typically are unreliable sources of food and would have been even more so for early hominids with their simpler technology. Plant foods, on the other hand, are more abundant, predictable, and require less energy

expenditure than animal foods. It is likely, therefore, that early hominids were mostly vegetarian with diets that varied in time and space
as opportunities permitted.

There is evidence that the hominid diet began changing during
the Middle Pleistocene era, around 700,000 years ago because they
then began hunting large land mammals and, later, more intensively
exploited marine foods such as shellfish, fish, and sea mammals.
Faunal remains and stone artifacts associated with ancestral Homo
erectus have indicated the spread of big game hunting, at this time,
from the original African sites into areas of Europe and Asia as well.
Except for those living in the very coldest climates, however, our ancestral hominids continued to depend largely on sources other than
meat from large animals for their subsistence (Gordon, 1987).

Woman as Tool Maker

Archaeological data cannot prove that ancestral hominids used
tools; however, studies of modern day primates suggest that they
did make and use tools. A "tool" is an object the user holds or carries,
and is used to alter the form or location of a second object. Among
primates, chimpanzees are the most accomplished tool users; they
regularly use tools for a variety of purposes: for feeding and drinking, as weapons, and as aids in bodily hygiene (Bascom, 1969). Most
tool use by chimpanzees is preceded by tool making, the modification of an inanimate object for more efficient use as a tool.[2] The most
common type of tools among chimpanzees are those used in connection with feeding or obtaining water. In addition to termiting, examples include: probes for obtaining ants or honey, stones used as
hammers to smash open tough-skinned fruits, seeds and nuts, and
leaf "sponges" to soak up water in tree holes (Goodall, 1968, 1973).
Studies have suggested that sex differences exist with respect to tool
use, as females were more likely to use tools in feeding.[3]

This sort of evidence suggests that ancestral hominids, with
hands freed of locomotor functions, made regular use of tools in connection with feeding and other activities. What kinds of tools? Who
made them? Stone tools in an archaeological context have not been
found in sites dating from two million years ago, more than one million years after the appearance of the first hominids. Tools made
from plant and organic materials, which are perishable and leave no

trace in the fossil or archaelogical record, also were likely to have been part of the early hominid tool kit.

Slocum (1975) has argued convincingly that slings or nets to carry babies might well have been among of the earliest human tools. Hominid mothers, lacking the body hair of their ancestral forebears, used these devices to secure their infants as they went about their food gathering tasks; these slings also served as containers when transporting food back to the home base. It is significant that, among contemporary hunter-gatherers, the kaross for carrying children and gathered foods is an essential part of every woman's tool kit. Containers for transport eventually would have led to containers for cooking and storage, and so probably were also invented by their female hominid users.

Among the earliest tools invented by hominids were digging sticks, another indispensable item in contemporary foraging women's tool kits. In the more open savanna habitats where the earliest hominids lived, a digging stick allowed the woman access to underground roots, insects, and small burrowing animals, thereby opening up new food resources. It is not difficult to imagine the transition from chimpanzees' "termiting" to homonids' invention of the digging stick. Early stone tools, such as hammerstones, scrapers, and choppers, usually regarded as hunting tools, also could have been used by women to gather and pulverize plant foods in preparation for eating.

What was women's role in tool-making? While it is impossible to tell who made what from the archaeological record, it is probable that both sexes made and used tools. The hominids' first tools, therefore, included the containers, digging sticks, and mortars and pestles invented by females in conjunction with their food gathering and child care activities.

Early Food Sharing

The transition from protohuman to human society required a significant change in subsistence activities from those based on individual foraging to communal foraging and food sharing. In hunting-gathering societies, both adult males and females brought food to their mates and dependents; the resultant group jointly consumed meals. A longer period of infant dependency for hominids, as compared to ancestral apes, meant that adults had to provide their infants food for increasingly longer periods after weaning.

Some anthropologists have suggested that food sharing between mother and infant has provided one link between solitary primate gathering and human food sharing. Chimpanzee adults rarely share plant foods; however mothers do share foods that are difficult to procure or prepare with their unweaned infants (McGrew, 1981). With the extended duration of infant dependency among humans, however, mothers began to increase the scope of their gathering to provide food for their still-dependent infants; the extension of the primate mother-infant bond only increased the depth and scope of social relationships (Slocum, 1975). This strong feeding bond between mother and infant most likely provided the first instance of food sharing among humans. In addition, Zihlman (1981) has suggested that early hominid females preferred and mated with social males who shared food with them and their offspring, eventually evolving them into a "pair bond" that the twentieth century refers to as a nuclear family.

Over time it clearly was culturally adaptive for food gathering activities to involve all mobile members of the group; this resulted in foraging a wider area that contained a greater variety of food resources. Ultimately all members shared in the bounty upon return to the base camp. When hunting large animals added a new dimension to the hominid subsistence patterns, the meat provided by the hunt was easily distributed on the basis of prior food sharing arrangements determined by the group's social network.

Contemporary hunting and gathering societies are of particular importance to anthropologists because they represent a way of life which represents, although it does not duplicate, that of ancient foragers since, for more than 99 percent of the period humans have existed as cultural creatures, they have lived as hunters and gatherers.[4] As the term suggests, these people support themselves by hunting, fishing, and gathering wild foods. Their technology is simple but effective, utilizing various types of spears, bows, arrows, digging sticks, knives, axes, fishing nets, and containers for collecting and transporting wild foodstuffs. These societies produce little or no surplus beyond subsistence needs; yet the diets of foragers are sufficient to meet their needs, and usually are more varied and nutritious than the diets of farming people.

Two basic assumptions dominate contemporary field work with hunting-gathering societies: they live in small groups, and they move around alot (Lee and deVore, 1968). Nearby small groups, however, are connected through visiting and marriage alliances. In a hunting and gathering context, people utilize a wide range of kinship ties to maintain flexible residential arrangements, organize work, and share food. One's kindred are potential resources in any number of ways.

This model, gleaned from contemporary foraging societies, provides a glimpse of prehistoric foraging societies that have existed throughout the long pre-agricultural past; it has suggested that the most compelling evidence of foraging as a successful means of adaptation may have been its extraordinary persistence over time.

Sexual Division of Labor

What models exist for reconstructing female and male roles during the long period of pre-agricultural life? One model, derived from contemporary hunter-gatherer societies has suggested a sexual division of labor in which hunting large land and sea mammals was almost exclusively a male activity, while gathering was mainly women's work. On the basis of this model, anthropologists have proposed various explanations for the evolution of this sex-differentiated behavior.

Most commonly they argue that while pregnancy and child care could have been combined with gathering activities, it would have been difficult to combine these tasks with hunts for large animals. Furthermore, big game hunting often required arduous long distance tracking of animals, and sometimes required considerable physical strength—both difficult for a pregnant or lactating woman to sustain. Precision in spearing animals or using a bow and arrow would have been difficult for someone carrying a physical burden; the presence of an infant or young child would also have been disruptive during the hunt. Because females in hunting and gathering societies spent most of their adult lives pregnant or nursing, it would have been a waste of the group's resources to spend time and energy training females to hunt. Furthermore, carrying large amounts of vegetable foods would have limited the woman's ability to pursue large game, just as pregnancy and child care interfered with hunting. Unlike hunting, gathering activities could have been readily combined with pregnancy and lactation. Therefore it was adaptive to practice a division of labor whereby some adults concentrated on hunting and others on gathering. Given the fact that only females are involved in pregnancy and lactation, it was functionally adaptive to assign females to gathering and males to hunting large game (Friedl, 1975, 1978; O'Kelly, 1980).

Some anthropologists, however, have been skeptical of these contemporary attempts to project the social organization and sex roles of contemporary hunting peoples back upon early hominid populations. They have argued that hunting arose relatively late in evolution, growing out of a technological and social basis in gathering, and may not have existed for more than 100,000 years (Zihlman, 1981). Furthermore, they question whether big game hunting was done exclusively by males. While it might have been common to exclude females in advanced pregnancy and nursing mothers from long distance hunting, other females might have participated in hunts (Harris, 1975). Ethnographic studies have verified the widespread practice of collective hunting involving both women and men. These studies also have even suggested that in some groups the role of "woman the hunter" was not insignificant (Estioko-Griffin and Griffin, 1975).

Ultimately we will never know when, and under what conditions, a sexual division of labor first emerged in the evolutionary record, or whether it did indeed begin with hunting. Most likely early hominids did not restrict subsistence activities to one sex; both males and females would have hunted and gathered. Big game hunting often involved techniques such as the stampede and surround which would have required active participation of most all the community. From an evolutionary perspective, both sexes made and used tools, shared food, cooperated in child care, lived in small-scale communities, and moved around a lot as do contemporary nomads.

Women in ancient foraging communities, as in modern ones, contributed substantially to the food supply. As Martin and Voorhies (1975) have concluded, both then and now "the only nonproducers were dependent young, adults near death, and invalids" (p. 175). The predominance of gathering activities over hunting in contemporary foraging societies and the fact that women most often were responsible for provisioning these foods both suggest that women have fulfilled a dominant economic role in both past and present hunter-gatherer societies.

Early Hominid Cuisine

In their entertaining smorgasbord of anthropological food tidbits, Farb and Armelagos (1980) have delineated four elements involved in any cuisine: the choice of foods for consumption, consistency in manner of food preparation, use of traditional principles when flavoring staple foods, and the existence of rules governing food custom, such as number of meals eaten, with whom they are eaten, ceremonial use of food, and food taboos. Their observation that "many small choices about eating, made over the centuries, indeed through the millenia, eventually produce a distinctive cuisine" (p. 228) is as true for the Mbuti hunters and gatherers of the Ituri forest as for members of any contemporary culture.

Early hominids selected foods from a wide variety of nutrients available within their ecological niche. Their diet was primarily vegetarian. According to Farb and Armelagos, two types of food were most palatable for humans: those having the texture and taste of meat, and those with the odor and vivid colors typical of fruit. Additionally neutral tasting foods, such as leaves, roots, seeds, and shoots, provided evolving humans with all the nutrients they needed. The high value placed on meat in contemporary foraging societies appears to support Farb and Armelagos' tasty meat theory. Further support has come from Lee's (1979) observation that, while it would be possible for the Bushman to exist entirely on vegetal foods, life for them would be boring without the excitement of meat feasts. Consequently they "eat as much vegetable food as they need, and as much meat as they can" (p. 41). Similar sorts of preferences characterize other known hunter-gatherer societies. Scarce meat, when obtained by hunters, is highly valued and correlates with the somewhat higher status of men as compared to women in these otherwise highly egalitarian societies. It is significant that societies in which both males and females participate in hunting, fishing, and gathering activities, such as the Mbuti, are characterized by the most egalitarian gender roles.

Early hominids developed various treatments for vegetable and animal products to extend their food choices beyond the more limited variety available to their primate forebears. Initially foods were eaten uncooked. Certain mechanical processing, such as opening hard shell seeds and nuts before eating, originally was accomplished with crude stone tools, but later with metates (pestles) and mortar-type tools. In this context, Lee (1979) has noted that the mortar and pestle was a tool almost equal to fire in significance. The !Kung used them for pounding and mixing different foods together. Pulverizing nuts, and mixing them with meat, roasted roots, and leafy greens helped prevent constipation and provided a very interesting flavor combination. Some food staples, such as acorns consumed by California Indians, and cycad (a type of seed-bearing plant similar to a palm tree) eaten by Australian foragers, were made edible by extracting harmful ingredients.

A human preference for cooked food probably developed gradually over a long period of time as its advantages came to be known. Cooking, in addition to tenderizing foods, destroyed bacteria and parasites in foods. Certain plant foods were more easily digested if cooked first. Others, poisonous when eaten raw, became edible when processed by drying, soaking, or cooking. Broken down by heat, the starch in plant foods changed chemically into more easily digested sugars. As Farb and Amelagos (1980) have noted, cooking amounts to a sort of "external predigestion." All known foraging societies have some means of cooking foods: be it roasting food over coals in earth ovens; boiling it in pots, shells, wood, baskets, or hides directly over the fire; or heating it with hot stones. The process of roasting, or applying heat from a fire directly to food, is very ancient; archeological remains of Homo erectus at Choukoutien caves in China have indicated that meat was roasted there 500,000 years ago. Traces of hearths apparently used for roasting dating from approximately the same time period have also been found in southern France and Hungary.

In the environments inhabited by earliest hominids, vegetable resources could be obtained anytime, so there was no need to preserve or store food. In fact food storage in most tropical areas is difficult because of the heat and humidity. In more temperate climates where vegetation was seasonal, game migrated and fish runs were more variable; consequently people were motivated to invent techniques for the preservation and storage of foods. Such cultural innovations permitted occupation of higher latitudes which early hominids had been able to inhabit earlier only during warm interstadial periods (Carpenter, 1942). The move into higher latitudes may have precipitated an increase in women's work when compared to life at lower latitudes where food preservation and storage was unnecessary.

Meanwhile Back at the Camp

In addition to their work procuring food and caring for children, what else did early hominid females do for work? What was their relationship to food? Most likely women's work included the preparation of food for their families, work shared by women the world over. Wells and Sim (1987) have succinctly summarized women's bond with food: "Their connection with sustenance starts when their body nourishes the unborn child inside them; it continues as their body bears milk for the baby at the breast and it ends with them being expected to provide food for everyone else, nearly all of the time" (p. 29).

It has been said that the closer the food is to the table the more it is women's work. Among contemporary hunter gatherers, the grinding of seeds, pounding of roots, and cooking of vegetable foods are done by women. Men butcher and cook meat, but nowhere are women wholly excluded from routine cooking. This practice may be explained by the fact that cooking is required to make many roots and seeds digestible for humans, particularly for young children. As collectors of these foods, it would be logical for women to continue the process of making these foods edible for their families.

When analyzing hunter-gatherer societies, anthropologists have noted that food processing and cooking are activities which could be done close to the home, and which involved repetitive tasks that could easily be interrupted and resumed: tasks compatible with pregnancy and child care. In contrast male activities sometimes required long absences from home and travel over great distances. This division of labor does not, however, mean that women were homebound; in fact gathering foodstuffs involved travel over considerable distances. Among the !Kung, for example, women's subsistence work, visits, and group moves require an adult woman to walk an average of 1,500 miles during the course of one year, much of the time carrying substantial burdens of food, water or material goods in addition to carrying each of her children under the age of four years (Lee, 1979). The !Kung recognize the plight of women with high fertility in their truism, "a woman who gives birth like an animal to one offspring after another has a permanent backache"

(p. 312). Given these high costs, it is not surprising that women who live as nomads typically space their children about four years apart; this low birth rate is partially explained by the fact that lactation usually causes infertility while the mother is breastfeeding her child.

How hard did women in these prehistoric foraging communities work? How difficult or easy was it to make a living? The popular notion that life was precarious and unpredictable for Paleolithic people is not supported by anthropological research. The demands of nomadic life limit the accumulation of wealth, and food surpluses generally do not exist; but the environment itself is the storehouse. Because they know what to expect, people see little point in accumulating food and other material goods beyond those required for their immediate needs. Production was geared almost entirely for use value rather than for exchange. Within this context, Sahlins (1972) has referred to hunter-gatherers as the "original affluent society" in that needs were limited, and people were able to meet their needs with only a few hours of work a day, "their labor chronically punctuated by days of slack, not to mention sleep" (p. 58). Studies of hunter-gatherers widely separated in time and space have revealed that people generally spent two to four hours a day in subsistence activities. What about other food-related activities? Study of the !Kung has revealed that women worked on average slightly less than two hours per day in food gathering activities; about three hours at housework including food processing, preparation, and cooking; overall, about the same as men, six hours per day (Lee, 1979).

Show Them That You Care

The evolutionary roots of women's roles in food sharing have been noted earlier in this chapter. Further evidence is provided by contemporary hunters and gatherers who participate in a variety of food exchanges: between men and women, usually involving an exchange of meat for vegetable foods; between men; and between women and other women, children, and the elderly. In all hunter-gatherer societies, in addition to procuring raw food, the processing and cooking of that food involved women in different social groups and exchange units. Women were almost always in charge of distributing cooked food from the hearth. These food exchanges were characterized by "generalized reciprocity," common to all hunter-gatherer societies. Givers expected no immediate return, and did not consciously calculate the value of the products or services involved. Outside of one's own household, generalized reciprocity usually took the form of specific obligations to certain kinfolk. Meat, particularly game too large for one family to consume immediately, was likely to be shared more widely than the more reliable vegetable foods. Since women primarily contributed vegetables to the food supply, they were less likely to be involved in elaborate networks of reciprocity. In fact, Friedl (1975) has argued that the practice of sharing meat served as the basis for whatever sexual inequality existed in hunting and gathering societies, even in those societies where food collected by women provided the bulk of members' daily food intake.

Draper (1975) has provided a counterpoint with her argument that the role !Kung women have played in food distribution has provided them with an important source of prestige. According to Draper, the distribution of meat was so circumscribed by social rules, as well as by the demands of camp members, that a hunter actually had little control over the meat he brought to camp. However, the female gatherer maintained control over the distribution of her foodstuffs when the gifts involved anyone outside her immediate family. !Kung women could make individual gifts of food to whomever they wished, usually relatives.

While it generally is difficult to ascertain from most past anthropologists' records exactly how women managed vegetable foods, in contrast to their elaborate descriptions of the rules for the distribution of meat, it would seem that control over the food they themselves had gathered provided women in these societies some measure of self-esteem. Food obtained by women was also shared with guests at family meals. Such hospitality presumably would augment one's self-worth in societies where generosity was esteemed as one of the highest virtues, and where "food offered in a generalized way, notably as hospitality, [was] good relations" (Sahlins, 1972, p. 216).

Summarizing their role in early hominid societies, women had major responsibilities in food production, preparation, and distribution. They invented, made, and used tools for food acquisition, food preparation, and transportation which, in turn, expanded the feeding and foraging strategies of early hominids and accommodated a growing range of habitats. The nature of the division of labor and the extent of male monopoly over hunting in these early societies varied in time and space, including several role permutations: women as big game hunters; independence of the sexes in food acquisition; and androgynous big game hunting by both sexes as well as communal gathering. However, in almost all societies, women's primary role would have been foraging for vegetable foods that served as the mainstay of the group's diet. Since women knew where the food was and as food sources were varied and abundant, there was little anxiety about food in these societies.

It is likely that women experienced lots of self-confidence regarding food acquisition.[5] Their relative degree of autonomy regarding food acquisition and individual control of labor production most likely provided hunter-gatherer women an additional source of self-esteem. Women were free to decide how to spend their day: whether to go gathering and with whom; whether to stay in camp, to visit neighbors, or to visit relatives in a more distant camp. They did not need the assistance of men to carry out their work. The personal autonomy of foraging women stands in marked contrast to the experience of women in more complex societies that have evolved over time.

What has been the experience of a typical woman in a foraging society? Shostack (1981) has recorded the ideal for !Kung women:

> To sit in front of your hut, pound mongongo nuts, cook meat in your fire, feed your older children and nurse your youngest, talk and laugh with visiting relatives, play music or participate in a trance dance . . . or just to sit alone with your husband after everyone has left, after your children are comfortably asleep—that is the way a woman's life should be. (p. 177)

Is it not reasonable to assume that early hominid women had a similar vision of happiness?

HORTICULTURAL SOCIETIES

In human societies one of the patterns that evolved out of a foraging way of life was horticulture: simple digging stick and hoe cultivation. Beginning around 10,000 years ago, hunters and gatherers in different parts of the world began to domesticate plants and animals. For the first time human communities gained control over the reproduction of plants and animals instead of depending on nature. This was a gradual process as late Stone Age hunters and gatherers experimented with cultivating wild foods and feeding animals near their settlements. From the centers where it began, the system spread into a wide variety of environments incorporating many different kinds of domesticants. Eventually this time of revolutionary food production—the Neolithic period—would introduce more changes than all the previous years of cultural evolution, setting the stage for the development of cities and states as well as modern civilizations.

There are a number of salient differences between societies dependent on foraging and those dependent on horticulture. The higher productivity guaranteed by farming provided the basis for more permanent, larger, and more dense populations. Horticultural people have exchangeable forms of wealth in land, stored food, and domestic animals. Organized warfare for the purpose of defending or expanding territories is endemic to these societies. All create situations demanding new kinds of social arrangements including: larger and more complex kinship groups; voluntary associations; and, in some cases, new forms of political integration (Friedl, 1975; Martin and Voorhies, 1975).

Prior to the colonial era, most non-western societies were horticultural. These "tribal" societies in North and South America, the Pacific Islands, Africa south of the Sahara, and parts of Asia have been studied extensively by anthropologists. They vary tremendously; in fact anthropologists traditionally have used comparisons among horticultural societies to demonstrate cultural diversity and the great variety possible in sex role behavior. However, amidst all these variations, some cross-cultural consistencies have endured for women around food production and family feeding.

The earliest horticultural systems developed in the neolithic period, and resembled the slash-and-burn systems widely practiced today in tropical forests. Preparation for horticulture first required clearing and preparing the land by felling trees, cutting down the forest underbrush, and burning the dried growth, the ashes from the fire providing the fertilizer. Gardens were planted with the aid of digging sticks or simple hoes which did not involve turning over the soil to any great depth. After a few years of cultivation, the land was fallowed for a number of years, allowing nutriments to return to the soil. This system required large tracts of land so that population densities remained low, although still higher than among most foraging societies. A more intense system of shifting cultivation was one in which the fallow was much shorter, perhaps only a couple of years. These more intensive systems required more labor per unit of land and, in turn, supported larger densities of population (Boserup, 1970).

Women's Work Is Never Done

Among all known horticulturalists, men have done the work involved in the preparation of land for cultivation: felling trees and cutting and firing the underbrush. Friedl (1975) has argued convincingly that the assignment of men to the initial clearing of land originated to fulfill the following needs: for defense of the land against invaders, for combat to obtain new land, and for hunting opportunities in virgin territory. Interestingly the most dangerous field-clearing tasks were often assigned to the more expendable members of the group: young males. Once the land was cleared, there was no adaptive advantage in having either females or males perform cultivating tasks; therefore a variety of labor patterns developed. It may be, however, that among the earliest horticulturalists, females were the primary cultivators just as they still are in many horticultural societies today.

It has been surmised that late Stone age people initially began to cultivate a few crops to supplement food collecting, hunting, and fishing. Eventually the growth in population compelled them to rely more heavily on cultigens and to develop more intensive systems of cultivation. Martin and Voorhies (1975), have examined a crosscultural sample of horticultural societies and found that the sexual division of labor was related to the degree of cultivation. Women monopolized cultivation in societies with low dependence on crops; greater dependence on cultigens was associated with a corresponding increase in the proportion of males engaged in cultivation activities. These anthropologists have speculated that gardening developed as a gradual elaboration of women's gathering activities. A monopoly on cultivation by women was retained in situations of low productivity; as the proportion of cultigens in the diet increased, however, women enlisted the labor of males.

As in foraging societies, a domestic mode of production characterized early horticultural societies. Although technology did allow for some accumulation of food and other goods, there were no large surpluses. People produced enough to satisfy their needs and then stopped working. This meant that no individual worked very hard. Studies of contemporary slash-and-burn subsistence farmers, who are actually present-day horticulturalists, have revealed that most people spend between three to six hours per day in subsistence activities; work days are interspersed with periods of leisure. As Sahlins (1972) dryly described this pattern: "Work is unintensive, intermittent and susceptable to all manner of interruption and impediments ranging from heavy ritual to light rainfall" (p. 86).

Women's work in horticultural societies included, in addition to their subsistence activities, food preparation, cooking meals, and child care—a pattern similar to that of foraging societies. However compared with foraging women, horticultural women worked more intensively in food processing and preparation. In many societies the work of pounding root crops and grinding corn or other grains required an additional two or three hours each day.[6]

The Importance of Family

With the development of horticulture and settled village life, land became a strategic resource, that is a base for food production, and not just an area where natural resources were exploited. Anthropologists have noted that in contemporary horticultural societies, uncleared land is available to anyone who wants to claim it; cleared land, however, is held communally by kin groups who maintain corporate ownership of the land and other resources.

The most common, simple forms of unilineal descent are patrilineality, where descent is traced through the male line, and matrilineality, where descent is traced through the female line. Anthropologists have noted that, while patrilineal kin systems predominate overall, matrilineality has been more common among horticulturalists than in any other type of society.[7] Various explanations have been offered as to why this is so; however, conclusions remain tentative. Rules for descent-reckoning, especially as they are combined with residence rules for a married couple, have had a bearing on male and female role configurations and the organization of domestic life in prehistoric horticultural societies in the more recent past.

In matrilineal systems with matrilocal residence, adult males must leave their own kin group at marriage and take up residence with their spouse. Related men are dispersed throughout a number of uterine groups which they enter as strangers. Since matrilineal-

ity/matrilocality divides the male fighting force, this living arrangement promotes peace and stability; men usually are associated with
warfare and a resultant denigration of women. This arrangement
also promotes female collective work; mothers, daughters, and sisters stay together throughout their lives. Female solidarity through
collective work, common residence, and ownership patterns usually results in greater power for the female members of society (Martin and Voorhies, 1975).

The indigenous culture of the Iroquois Indians of upstate New
York, for example, has provided an interesting account of the ways
matrilineality and matrilocality in combination with economic control led to significant economic and political power for these native
Americans (see Morgan, 1962; Brown, 1970). The Iroquois, a confed-
eracy of several related tribes, had a system of matrilineal kin
groups. They lived in a highly favorable and stable environment
subsisting on a varied diet of cultivated foods, fish, and game.
Males were occupied mainly with warfare against distant tribes, in
effect, community control was relegated to the women who organized around a core comprised of mother, daughters, and sisters in
matrilocal residence. Property passed through the female line as related women formed life-long residential groups as well as kinship
units. Crucial in consolidating the power of the women was the family longhouse, a large structure of bark and wood containing many
compartments, each occupied by a family. The authority of the
household rested with the matron who ruled supreme within the
longhouse. Brown (1970) has argued convincingly that the key to the
high status for Iroquois women lay in the control they exercised over
the food supply. The food supply and the distribution of food, both
within and among households, was controlled entirely by women,
including even the food from the men's hunt.

In patrilineal/patrilocal systems, women left their kin groups
when they married, moving into the household and lineage of the
husband. Because women in the household came from different villages, there was less inclination to work cooperatively as compared to
matrilineal/matrilocal groups. In polygynous societies, however,
co-wives regularly cooperated with each other. Anthropologists have
noted that patrilineal systems appear to have been most adaptive in
circumstances where greater productivity was valued and where
critical resources were scarce. In contrast, matrilineal systems were
more compatible with habitats in which resources were adequate or

in excess of the population's needs, and where competition between communities was minimal. Such conditions largely have disappeared in the modern world. A sequence of change, wherein matrilineal systems were replaced by more expansive exploitative, patriliny, have been well documented in ethnographic literature. This sequence suggests that matriliny was more prevalent in earlier horticultural societies. Regardless of the distant past, in more recent times, patriliny has prevailed among kin-based societies, just as it always has among advanced horticultural societies. Correspondingly, these societies are male-dominant and contrast with the more egalitarian sex roles found among foragers and many matrilineal horticulturalists.

What's Mine May Be Yours

As horticultural societies evolved, food production intensified, and resulted in greater production and more complex techniques of food processing and storage. The transformation from production of foodstuffs for direct consumption to production of surpluses for exchange involved women and men in previously undifferentiated economic spheres. Simple horticultural societies, as in foraging societies, produced food for subsistence, and exchange was based on reciprocity. The ability to organize kin to produce food and to manage and control surpluses involved political forms unknown among egalitarian foragers or simple horticulturalists. Much has been written, for example, about the Melanesian "big man" redistributor who achieved status by hosting public feasts. Likewise, northwest coast native chiefs competed for status via redistributive feasts known as potlatches. Societies geared to surplus production develop dual economies: one set of activities associated with subsistence and another set associated with accumulation and exchange.

In this arrangement, women's work was geared to meet household needs, while men's work involved them in social production for exchange. It is significant that while women continued their role as primary cultivators, they now were excluded for the most part from extra-domestic economic and political leadership. Women could not become "big men" or Kwakiutl chiefs. These societies began a male/female role dichotomy that became the standard in more complex agricultural societies. As Martin and Voorhies (1975) have noted, this shift in the balance of power gradually resulted in the isolation of women from central roles in other societal institutions.

This need not have been the case. One basis for women's participation in extra-domestic exchange was through trade. The trading expertise of West African market women has been well documented in anthropological literature. Here women handled a large share of the trading; they participated both in local markets and long distance trade with other tribal groups. Women traders not only sold their own horticultural produce and other items but they also bought supplies from other women for resale. Their profits from trading enabled them to engage in various forms of extra-domestic distribution. In Nigeria, for example, Ibo women could acquire honorific titles or buy "wives" to take over domestic work and child care. Yoruba women distributed wealth derived from trading as a way to organize or join women's religious cult societies (Bascom, 1969). It is significant that, in these societies, a woman's relations with her husband and co-wives were considered secondary to her relations with the outside world. The Caribbean, North and South America, and Southeast Asia are other areas where women historically have played an important role in trading.

A second basis for women's participation in distribution involved inherited positions of rank. Mothers, sisters, and daughters of chiefs or kings exercised power to command resources and arrange distributions as, for example, among royal women in advanced horticultural societies in Africa, for example, the Bemba and in Polynesia, the Tonga (Friedl, 1975).

From an evolutionary perspective, the exclusion of women from controlling land and resource allocation and redistributive networks represented a fundamental change in relations between the sexes. In most patrilineal horticultural societies, women were primary cultivators, but their relationship to land and food resources was a consequence of marriage rather than descent. Likewise in societies geared toward production for exchange, women's (and men's) work intensified to the extent that household assets were mobilized for surplus production. One way to increase household productivity was to increase the work force by polygyny. In the words of one Melanesian leader, "another woman go garden, another woman go take firewood, another woman go catch fish, another woman cook him—husband he sing out plenty people come kaikai [eat]" (Landtman, 1927, p. 168, as quoted in Sahlins, 1972, p. 136).

Despite revolutionary changes in the social organization of production and distribution, women's role in relation to food remained essentially unchanged from Neolithic times until the industrial revolution. Prehistoric horticultural women, like their contemporary counterparts, cultivated crops and cared for animals, processed and prepared food, and continued to feed their families. They managed the domestic distribution of food and were in charge of dispensing hospitality and gifts of food to their kin. Did they derive autonomy and self-esteem from these activities? Most likely they did.[8]

Control and management of food once it had been brought into the household was usually a woman's task, and this could provide a source of power and prestige. Bemba women, for example, were admired for their industry and resourcefulness in finding food in the bush; it was both a right and duty to control the use of stored grain, to know at what rate it should be consumed, and what amount of food to cook to honor her husband's guests. Through the distribution of food she demonstrated generosity and gained popularity within her community (Richards, 1939).

Despite differences between the two types of societies, it is important to note that there was continuity in women's important roles as food producers and providers even as foragers evolved into horticulturalists. Even in societies where male dominance was most entrenched, women's activities continued to be valued. Certainly these activities provided a sense of self-worth and confidence just as they had in foraging societies. The dichotomy of worker versus wife and mother, typical of Western societies with an agrarian tradition, did not exist among horticultural people; their experience demonstrated the interdependency of these roles. When one anthropologist asked contemporary Gikuyu women in Kenya "what are your most important roles?" Wanjiku, a woman in her eighties, gave a typical response:

> The most important roles are, first, to take care of the husband and at the same time, care for my children. . . . But equal with these is my role as a farmer—taking the cows to river to drink and feeding them taking a kibanga [machete] to the shamba to cultivate and from the shamba carrying home firewood for the cooking fire. They are all one they cannot be separated. (Davison, 1996, p. 73)

AGRARIAN SOCIETIES

As the populations in horticultural communities increased in relation to available resources, people were motivated to search out new techniques to increase crop yields and maintain the continuous fertility of their fields. Increased population density made it impossible to continue with a system requiring long fallow periods with large amounts of land left uncultivated. The evolutionary transition to more intensive systems of land use went hand-in-hand with a shift from cultivation by means of fire, axe, and hoe to plough agriculture (Boserup, 1970). Agriculture involves the use of ploughs, draft animals, manure, and irrigation. These additions when working the land triggered some remarkable cultural achievements: cities, states, and modern civilization among the most notable.

The development of advanced cultivation techniques appears to have occurred independently in a limited number of areas in the old and new worlds: southeast and southwest Asia; northeast Africa; Central America; and the Andean highlands. Earliest known archaeological centers appeared first in Mesopotamia and Egypt around 3000 B.C. Out of these precedents arose the great agrarian civilizations of Greece, Rome, Egypt, and China. Widely hailed as the "dawn of civilization," the agricultural revolution brought with it an overall loss of status and power for women in relation to men; a similar positioning occurred for the majority of the population in relation to a tiny ruling class (O'Kelly, 1980).

The level of productivity achieved through plow agriculture allowed for the production of vast food surpluses unknown among horticultural societies. For the first time, large segments of the population were freed from primary food production. This impetus saw the rise of large urban centers, occupational specializations, and complex military-government structures. Agrarian societies created highly developed class systems. Most of the population were now peasants, or preindustrial food-producers who paid rent or taxes. These societies were also characterized by marked sexual stratification; the subordination of women actually has been most intense in agrarian societies.[9]

Life Becomes "Inside-Outside"

Why did women lose their productive role with the transition to agriculture? What were the social consequences of the "nonproducer" role? Anthropologists have observed that agricultural labor involves clearing land, plowing, caring for draught animals, and digging irrigation ditches; all of these tasks require great muscular strength, longer hours, and frequent travel away from home; all also are incompatible with pregnancy and child care. It is significant that, despite the higher yields, agricultural work was so much more demanding that horticulturalists in many parts of the world resisted the new economic arrangement. Agriculture virtually eliminated the need for weeding, a time-consuming task traditionally assigned to women. This was an important change since all horticultural women had participated in farm work; in fact, the labor force often was predominantly female. But agricultural women were exempted from the fields, except during the harvesting of crops; then even children worked the fields.

The transition to agriculture was accompanied by changes in land tenure: from corporate kin groups to individual ownership, from communal ownership to private property. As a result, unlineal kinship groups that characterized the horticultural arrangement gave way to bilateral kinship systems. Kin-based production groups decreased in size and complexity as smaller domestic groups based on monogamy and separate (neolocal) residence replaced extended family and polygynous households. When males became the primary cultivators, polygyny declined as multiple wives became a liability rather than an asset.

These changes in the sexual division of labor and in household composition gave rise to what Martin and Voorhies (1975) have termed the "inside-outside" dichotomy: A "conceptual distinction of domestic and extradomestic labor [which] had the effect of isolating the sexes from one another, and women from public life" (p. 290). This domestic/public dichotomy of women's and men's work gave men control of the political and economic structures. Originally begun in agrarian class societies, this power arrangement has continued into the present.

Continuity and Change in Women's Work[10]

The establishment of agrarian patriarchal societies originated during the period from about 3000 to 600 B.C. By 1000 B.C. early societies were located around the Mediterranean, and fed into what eventually became the tradition of the Western World. Historical accounts of ancient Greece, Rome, and Medieval Europe have revealed that societies widely separated in space and time still were remarkably consistent in their maintenance of the public/domestic dichotomy that reinforced female subordination. In Medieval Europe, for example, under a feudal system of agriculture, a peasant woman managed the household but her activities outside the home were restricted. The husband controlled goods and property, so his wife was expected to be subservient in every way. She served him at mealtimes and stood behind his chair while he ate; she herself ate only after all the men in the household were done eating.

Peasant men were connected to the market and, therefore, the outside world since their crops and labor had exchange value. Their women, however, though restricted from the outside world of the market, were not entirely absent from home. Agrarian women also served as a reserve labor supply during peak periods of planting and harvesting. Their involvement with field crops, however, was greatest during harvesting when, as the "manufacturers" of men's labor, they processed and preserved food, brewed intoxicants, and did the usual weaving, sewing, and baking expected of them.

Yet women also continued their own production, frequently satisfying nearly all their family's food requirements from their gardens and the animals they cared for, such as chickens, goats, pigs. Overall the higher yields and seasonal nature of agricultural production meant that agricultural work was much more labor intensive for both women and men when compared with horticultural systems. The widespread belief that "civilization" was associated with an increase in "leisure time" is a myth; on the contrary for the great majority of the population, higher productivity was associated with increased amounts of work in crop production. This was even more true for women who now were engaged in more intensive work in all food-related activities.

From the end of the Roman Empire, feudal agriculture dominated in most Western societies until this form of economic production was superseded by capitalist trade and commerce (eleventh through the sixteenth centuries).

Colonial United States

In seventeenth century pre-industrial England and France, economic life was organized around family economies and consisted of small farms and shops. Domestic production in these homes certainly continued the sexual division of labor by sex, but no concomitant distinction existed between family life and production for income (Tilly and Scott, 1987). When Europeans invaded America they brought along these traditions to the New World. A family economy based on individual ownership of private property certainly could not have differed more from native Americans' kin-based communal ownership of land.

Throughout the Americas, native women raised corn, beans, and squash, known as the "three sisters." Among the horticultural tribes of New England, three-sisters agriculture provided staple foodstuffs. Women played the major role in planting and distributing these crops (Merchant, 1989). In the 1600s, for example, Roger Williams described Native American women's high yields of corn: "The woman of the family will commonly raise two or three heaps of twelve, fifteen, or twenty bushels a heap which they dry in round broad heaps; and if she have help of other children and friends, much more" (as quoted in Merchant, 1989, p. 80). Women's multi-cropping system for growing corn, beans, and squash provided nutritional advantages in addition to enormous yields. The procedure involved planting maize (corn) and beans in hills whereby the maize plants provided support for climbing beans. Squash, planted between the hills, provided a cover to keep weeds down and moisture retained. More recent studies in agricultural science have judged the corn-bean-squash triad to be both nutritionally and ecologically sound.

European settlers in America learned the advantages of this system of planting from native women; now they also could cultivate maize without extensive land clearing or plowing. Native American women also taught the Europeans how to prepare corn cakes and porridge, survival foods for their first years in a strange new environment. The European colonists, however, had little sympathy for the female farming systems that sustained them during their first years in America and eventually reverted to their old system of agricultural production. The three sisters were usurped by macho European cropping systems. Instead of using hoes, for example, colonial men used plows and oxen to clear the fields and plant single crops in rows. Though their European traditions bred disdain for woman's participation in the field work, colonial men realized the need for additional labor. Therefore both men and women worked in the fields (Sachs, 1996).[11]

As a result, in rural communities along the eastern seaboard from roughly 1600 to 1820, colonists went about their daily life in the manner of their European forebears. The sexual division of labor essentially recreated the inside/outside dichotomy established by the agrarian tradition. Men worked in the fields growing corn, barley, and wheat for cash crops. Colonial housewives were expected not only to prepare and serve meals, but to provide much of the food for their families. Women, in fact, were more important in providing subsistence for the farm family than were men.[12]

Settling North America with family farms (plantations in the south) enabled America to expand its territorial and economic interests. Those implementing this practice were oblivious to its concomitant destruction of Native American peoples and cultures. By 1850 in the eastern part of America, privately owned family farms had destroyed and replaced native horticultural systems in the eastern states; descendants of these European farmers later repeated this pattern of destruction across the continent. The three sisters, however, along with a wide variety of other cultigens, remained an important portion of the Colonial diet.

Later the commercial production and milling of wheat shifted interest away from homegrown corn.

Wheat eventually replaced corn as a staple, except in the south, and Indian corn became mere animal fodder. It is interesting to note that, throughout the world, corn is a staple consumed mainly by poor people.[13] Wheat, served as bread, has endured as a symbol of the elite.

Work Gives Meaning to Life

Although colonial housewives were limited geographically in their domain, they were not isolated; but neither were they self-sufficient. This reality required colonial women to develop another array of skills since families often found it necessary to bargain for needed goods and services. Ulrich's (1991) examination of New England women's housekeeping activities during the period 1650–1750 has revealed the complexity and skill required to perform these duties. In colonial New England, for example, there was no central retail trade, so procuring ingredients for dinner involved many transactions. To support their families, farm women likewise were obliged to trade or barter vegetables from their gardens, surplus milk, dairy products, chickens, eggs, and other items they produced.[14]

Butter making, a traditional female task performed by women over the ages, was another important commodity on farms, providing income for women, food for the family, and a cushion against hard times. Elsewhere women in rural areas regularly raised and cared for domestic animals such as chickens, pigs, cows, goats, or sheep for home consumption or for the market. The value of such work has been expressed in a French peasant saying: "No wife, no cow, hence no milk, no cheese, neither hens, nor chicks, nor eggs" (Fox, 1980, p. 75). American farm women raised chickens for subsistence and extra income and also marketed surplus eggs. During hard economic times, especially during the depression years, women's egg money saved many farms when men's cash crops failed to provide necessary family income (Fink, 1986). It is noteworthy that farm women continued to raise chickens for "pin money" until the 1940s, when they were pushed out of the poultry market by large scale egg and broiler producers (Sachs, 1996).

The work women did in the fields, in their gardens, in trading activities, and a multitude of other tasks involved in feeding their families was essential to their survival and well-being. Certainly both women and men were "breadwinners" in the American family farm economy. Faragher's (1991) estimate that mid-nineteenth century midwestern American women were engaged in from one-third to one-half of all farm food production can be extrapolated backwards to colonial women and quite possibly to peasant women in other agrarian societies as well.

There is little evidence to suggest that men gave women's work a second thought; their hard work was simply taken for granted. While the farm could not exist without women's labor, these workers received minimal recognition for their work. This finding is no surprise, since the "male-provider female-domestic" division of labor that arose with intensive cultivation complemented an ideology in which male dominance emphasized and reinforced female subordination and inferiority. Women's important economic participation most often did not produce equality in gender roles either in practice or ideology. Shorter's (1976) studies of peasants in Western Europe, for example, have shown that, while women had considerable economic authority within the domestic economy, it did not generalize to other areas. Even though contributions to the farm's prosperity were absolutely essential, the sex roles allocated these farm women remained inferior and subordinate.

How did women view their work? What meaning did their work hold for them? Was it a source of self-esteem? On this matter the historical record is mostly silent. Women's voices have been muted, because they never were asked what work meant to them. Also they themselves accepted the dominant ideology that judged their contribution as merely adjunct to efforts made by the master of the house.[15]

In a more contemporary context, one researcher has recounted with amazement farm women's descriptions of the array and extent of their work which they then minimize as "helping" (Sachs, 1996). Such examples suggest that farm women have interpreted their experiences according to the dominant agrarian ideology which defined their positions simply as farm wives and mothers, whether in a French peasant village or colonial New England.

While they may have seen their field work as "helping" men, it is likely that the colonial and rural farm women did indeed derive a sense of value and worth from the work they did. The value of their work lay in the immediate usefulness of their products. The woman herself performed all necessary steps in the production of food, whether gardening, preserving, drying, or storing. The joys of women's work lay in the satisfaction or a sense of accomplishment derived from bread well made, butter nicely molded, beer well brewed, quilts intended for heirlooms. Men, on the other hand, worked in the fields where

> neither the corn nor the grain was immediately consumable but required processing; the connection between production and consumption-the full cycle of work-was not embodied in a man's own activity. The cyclical nature of farm woman's work might allow her to see in a flowering field of blue flax the linen for next summer's chemise. For men the fields would yield not usable, tangible articles—bread or hominy—but bushels; quantities not things. (Faragher, 1991, p. 131)

The saying, "a man may work from sun to sun, but a woman's work is never done," captures the inequity in the division of labor for farm women, and reminds us that such joys of women's work were bittersweet.

Camelot Remembered

For more than 99 percent of the time cultural beings have been on earth, they have existed as foragers. Humans subsisted on products derived from domesticated plants and animals for only a small portion of their existence. Therefore the period introduced by the agricultural revolution represents only a tiny slice of human history. Foraging was an extraordinarily successful way of life. In these societies women played an important economic role in food production and provision for their families. The predominance of women in subsistence activities was reflected in social arrangements characterized by sexual equality still unknown in today's advanced civilization. Women actually controlled food production in the earliest horticultural societies. But eventually farming was dominated by men, and along with this new system of agriculture came class and sexual stratification systems. Agrarian societies relegated females to secondary tasks and a domestic role in an "inside-outside" economy. Women, however, continued their crucial role as providers for their families; they made sure that palatable food appeared on the table at mealtimes. It is important to remember that, for most of the long history of human society, women's work was highly valued as were women workers. Only with the "dawn of civilization" did this sexual equality disappear.

Chapter 3

Subversion by Food Processors and Reformers

RISE OF THE GIANT FOOD PROCESSORS

In his insightful account of changes in American diet during the last hundred years, Levenstein (1988) has identified several factors that allowed for the rise of giant food processors at the close of the Civil War.[1] Once railroad systems had expanded to crisscross the country, production of basic foodstuffs was increasingly centralized around railway distribution points. Markets for wheat, corn, beef, hogs, sugar, dairy products, and fresh fruit and vegetables all were affected by this change in patterns of delivery to consumers. It was now possible to stockpile huge quantities of goods at central locations where processing facilities quickly materialized. For the housewife consumer, changes in production translated into lower prices for many of the basic foodstuffs she needed on a regular basis.

Stockpiling foodstuffs now required some processing of the food products to preserve them for the longer periods that lapsed between the actual production of a food and its actual consumption by the home consumer. For example, packaging soda crackers into individually wrapped packages under a brand name, as a replacement for the old soda cracker barrel in the general store, allowed the producer to claim "freshness" for his brand-name soda crackers while allowing him to charge more for the same basic product.

Americans' food preferences definitely were influenced by these production changes. One example of this phenomenon was a change in the general public's sugar preferences—from brown to white—as a result of a very successful advertising campaign by the American Sugar Refining Company. American consumers were persuaded that brown sugar contained questionable microbes, therefore causing dark sugar to be judged inferior to a more "refined" white sugar.

It is significant that, as the distance between the production of food and its actual consumption lengthened, individuals became increasingly concerned about "healthy" foods in their diet. Discovery of the existence of bacteria in the 1880s only excited the possibilities of "germs" in one's food in the imagination of the average American consumer. By the turn of the century, the middle classes had become very concerned about the link between food and good health. Kellogg's "Corn Flakes" and Post's "Grape-Nuts" and "Postum" are early examples of processed food marketed as health food.

Canning under steam pressure began on a large-scale basis in America during the 1870s. This technological breakthrough allowed for a wide variety of canned goods to be made available to consumers. A demand for factory canned foods over fresh or home canned food in Mason jars was shaped through a very effective advertising and marketing campaign by companies such as that of Henry Heinz in Pittsburgh. Heinz was able to persuade housewives that his factory-canned food was fresher and safer for consumption (fewer "germs") than the home-produced food housewives were serving their families prior to the advent of food processors. By 1900 the American food processing industry had become very big business, indeed, accounting for 20 percent of the nation's manufacturing.

And yet during the next few decades, at least some women resisted the pressure to use store-bought food rather than prepare their own "from scratch." Immigrant and rural women were most likely to continue to "put up" their own produce for off-season consumption.[2]

By the 1920s, however, most middle class American women really thought that, "armed only with a can opener, some Jell-O and a bottle of mayonnaise they could create wondrously healthy and easy meals for the family" (Levenstein, 1988, p. 167). Such an attitude was a far cry from the views of their mothers' generation of cooks. Food advertising that encouraged a consumer preference for processed food over fresh or home-produced food also caused the American housewife to doubt her own ability to adequately feed her family in terms of freshness, safety (from bacteria), taste, and cost. This sort of questioning on the part of housewives signaled the first major disruption of one of the basic tenets of women's traditional identity as providers, producers, and preparers of their family's food. As such, it represented a significant turning point in American women's relationships to food.

In her engaging account of women and cooking at the turn of the century, Shapiro (1986) has observed the link between the usurpation of women's traditional role in the kitchen and their increasing tendency to question their ability to know best how to nurture their family with food: "Between World War I and the 1960s, generations of women were persuaded to leave the past behind when they entered the kitchen, and to ignore what their senses told them while they were there" (pp. 215–16).

Fannie Farmer's advocacy of "level measurements" near the turn of the century quickly replaced cooking on the basis of individual judgment. The prior tradition of cooking by means of "a little of this and a little of that" had allowed cooks to vary ingredients on the basis of personal preference, availability of ingredients, and creative impulse. The new "scientific" approach of cooking schools such as Fannie Farmer's denied women the opportunity for self-expression in the preparation of food.[3] Combined with the mass availability of printed recipes, requiring precise measurements and specifying ingredients to be used, housewives' work in the kitchen had become one of "following directions" rather than trusting their own instincts, experience, and personal taste in the preparation of a dish.

A "SCIENTIFIC" APPROACH TO FOOD AND EATING

In addition to self doubts about one's adequacy in the kitchen as a result of mass marketing, working-class and immigrant households were being assaulted by food reformers who recommended that people select their foods on the basis of their chemical composition, rather than taste, appearance, or other considerations. People were being told to eat what was good for them rather than what they liked. An emphasis on the chemical composition of food as a basis for organizing and preparing meals discouraged the use of personal taste preferences and familial ethnic culinary traditions as criteria for determining family's meals.

Shapiro (1986) has commented that food reformers believed that "if they could reform American eating habits, they could reform Americans; and so, with the zeal so often found in educated, middle-class women born with more brains and energy than they were supposed to possess, they set about changing what Americans ate and why they ate it" (p. 5). It would take thirty or so years, however, for these culinary reformers to truly manifest their influence over the food preferences of the average American household.

Early efforts by food reformers, including Ellen Richards at the New England Kitchen and Fannie Farmer at the Boston Cooking School, failed to acknowledge the importance of the psychological role of food in American working-class and immigrant families. Working-class people associated upward mobility with the consumption of more meat, beef in particular. Immigrants and others with non-Anglo culinary traditions utilized tomatoes, potatoes, and other fruits and vegetables much more than the food reformers recommended. Richards and her colleagues, on the other hand, felt that white flour, condensed milk, and lots of refined sugar constituted a more proper basis for carbohydrate consumption.

The American middle class expanded tremendously in the 25 years after 1880, eagerly emulating the upper-class style of socializing with friends and business associates through dining. Entertaining over food, particularly at dinner parties, rapidly became one of the central features of middle-class social life. It placed additional pressure on middle-class housewives to expand their traditional role of mother and wife to become the hostess and social ally for their husbands—a phenomenon that also influenced acceptable body size through the early decades of the twentieth century. A famous restaurateur's comment during the 1920s, "a young man contemplating marriage no longer asks whether a girl is a good cook; he wants to know whether she is a good sport" (Levenstein, 1988, p. 164), indicates how far middle-class women's identity had drifted from a basic responsibility to feed and nurture family members.

The Servant Problem

Middle-class entertaining in the style of the upper class was further complicated by the "servant problem." Northern European immigrants and farm girls previously provided a cheap labor supply for the kitchen and dining room. The rapid growth of factories and offices in urban centers provided more interesting and financially rewarding work for poor young women formerly destined to become servants of the upper classes in the North. In the South, black cooks and house servants continued to play their historic roles. Outside the South, middle-class housewives were "reduced" to using transitory southern black, Asian, or immigrants from middle or eastern Europe as their domestic work force. As Levenstein (1988) observed, "this often meant that it was difficult for middle-class white Anglo-Saxon Protestants to find servants able to understand their orders, let alone understand their needs" (p. 63).

One solution was to train both the housewife and servant to treat housekeeping on a strictly scientific and business-like basis. This strategy only guaranteed to further alienate the middle-class housewife from the traditional nurturant and sensual qualities of food preparation, something working-class women were "allowed" to continue doing only until the home economics movement influenced their own cooking style through the efforts of nutritionists working both for the government and the schools their children attended.

Another so-called solution to the servant problem was the development of cooperative kitchens whereby several families collectively hired professional kitchen staff and took their meals together in a central location. This shortlived turn-of-the-century phenomenon revealed just how despicable food preparation had become even for women who did not directly prepare the food but rather directed the efforts of others in food preparation. "The tyranny of the kitchen," a phrase used by Catherine Selden to describe the growing loss of control over servants' activities by their employers, suggested the desperation middle-class women were feeling about their kitchens and their place within them.

Changes in Women's Role

It is significant that little attention was focused on this rupture in women's traditional food roles when food preparation and consumption were taken out of the home with the formation of "Bellamy Clubs," as the cooperative kitchens were called. Critics of the cooperative kitchens only regarded them as basically incompatible with the American ideal of family life. Reacting to Bellamy's proposals as described in a previous issue, one *Good Housekeeping* reader wrote that "the home is the unit whose integrity it behooves us to protect against every danger" especially against "the socialist doctrine of collectivism and cooperation" (Levenstein, 1988, p. 66). Such criticism totally ignored the disruption in social sex role that certainly occurred for the female head of household under this arrangement. Perhaps critics did not perceive that a married woman might have a role separate from her identity as part of the "family unit."

To solve the problem of maintenance of family life when the family's food was prepared at a central location, Selden suggested an early version of "take out" by having each family's food delivered to their home for private consumption. In response to this suggestion, Charlotte Perkins Gilman observed that the "process fails because . . . cooking and cleaning are not family functions. We do not have a family mouth, a family stomach. . . . Eating is an individual function. Cooking is a social function. Neither is in the faintest degree a family function" (Levenstein, 1988, p. 68). What is striking about this statement is Gilman's lack of a sense of "family" as the term is currently used. For Gilman and other social reformers at the turn of the century, problems of food preparation, cuisine, and food consumption seem to be viewed only from a rational, scientific perspective. There was no apparent consideration given to the importance of these "problems" within the context of women's socially defined role: one in which women were defined by their relationship to the family.

Radical experiments with elements of women's social sex role must have encouraged many middle-class women to seriously question the value, and even the necessity, of functions traditionally deemed part of their role within the home and community. Resolution of this issue was now out of the middle-class housewife's hands as "the very forces of capitalism which already had transformed so much of American life would now certainly take the simple, profitable step that (was) to follow" (Levenstein, 1988, p. 69). With the help of the home economics movement, capitalism would modernize American eating and housekeeping.

Motivation fueling the food reform movement has been interpreted differently by the two major scholars of this historic culinary period. Levenstein (1988) has suggested that housewives actually wanted release from their traditional role: "In their women's clubs, at their teas, they continued to conspire and experiment with ways to free themselves from the terrible burdens of the home while at the same time continuing to fulfill society's expectations of them" (p. 83). Shapiro (1986), however, has interpreted this movement as an expression of women's altruistic and utilitarian tendencies: "The women who founded and led the domestic-science movement were deeply interested in food, not because they admitted to any particularly intense appetite for it, but because it offered the easiest and most immediate access to the homes of the nation" (p. 5). Clearly Shapiro's emphasis was on social betterment, not personal satisfaction.

Both interpretations clearly indicated a desire to change society's expectation of appropriate matronly behavior. Both also suggested that women themselves no longer valued their traditional role of feeding and nurturing their families. Levenstein, however, has posited internal desires for change; when no external person or program could ultimately "save" the middle-class housewife from going into her own kitchen and cooking for her family, she resolved the problem by shifting to smaller and less elaborate meals. This reduction in the amount of food and number of courses served at the two major meals of the day created a lasting impact on eating styles (and acceptable body image) in American culture for at least the next century. Yet even the middle-class remained "robust eaters" until World War I when the impact of food reformers and newer definitions of acceptable body image finally were firmly established in American culture.

By the 1920s the middle class definitely was less interested in food as competing loyalties to peer groups and new leisure activities plus the tendency to "eat and run" became acceptable family behavior. Family members also were eating at different times to accommodate their other social obligations. Housewives were aware of the nutritional compromises they made when preparing a meal from various cans of food quickly assembled into a visually attractive meal as compared to the more time-consuming preparation of meals "from scratch" made by their mothers (or their mothers' servants). Fresh products were correctly identified by consumers in a 1926 Department of Commerce survey to have superior flavor and nutritional composition. The same consumers acknowledged, however, that canned foods were more convenient. It is clear that sky-rocketing sales of canned and other prepared foods in the 1920s were fueled by millions of individual decisions to sacrifice taste, and even nutrition, in exchange for reduced preparation time.

The loss of nutritional content associated with this "modern" style of cooking left a legacy women still deal with today: the increasingly reported phenomenon that food does not satisfactorily nourish the individual, leaving her with cravings for more food, even after consuming an entire meal comprised of processed food. It probably was no accident that "diet" and a discussion of calories first became a topic for American women's magazines during the same time period in which the middle-class first began consuming large amounts of processed foods.

One of the pioneers of domestic science, Ellen Richards, went so far as to query, "must we not make them dissatisfied?" in her consideration of ways to engage American women in her movement. Keeping women dissatisfied was necessary, Richards felt, if "the new function of the twentieth-century housekeeper was to consume" (Shapiro, 1986, p. 177). A woman who was hungry, even after consuming an entire meal, clearly felt dissatisfied.[4]

Assault on Immigrant and Middle-Class Kitchens

By the turn of the century, food reformers were not content with their limited success in changing middle-class eating habits. After all, food reformers' first efforts involved attempts to manipulate the food served in working-class and immigrant households beginning in the 1890s New England Kitchen. The attitude of early food reformers had been that, regardless of class, it always was the housewife who was to blame; as stated by a prominent New York journalist in the early 1890s, "half the drunkenness that makes so many homes miserable is at least encouraged, if not directly caused, by mismanagement and bad cooking at home" (Levenstein, 1988, p. 99).

When literature on eating customs in the early decades of the twentieth century is examined, however, it is clear that, even though the assault on diet included the working and middle classes, it was a particular attack on the diet of newer immigrant groups. American families of British and north European origin were eating quite a varied (if meat-heavy) diet. It was the Italian, Jewish, Slavic, and other central and eastern European housewives who seemed particularly resistant to dietary change and, therefore, were targeted as most resistant to change. These immigrant women often took great pride not only in their cooking skills, but also in their ability to cook economically; food and cooking were central elements in the role housewives from these immigrant groups fulfilled. In a particularly insensitive way, food reformers felt that the American-born worker's diet was fine; the problem was simply to help the foreign-born adopt this diet. This attitude reflects early food reformers' tendency to ignore what they could have learned from immigrants. Their emphasis remained to change the food preferences of America's newest citizens.[5]

After the turn of the century, food reformers changed strategy; they realized that if the older female head of the household was too "difficult" or "slow" to change her food behavior, then assimilation might best be served by molding the food preferences of her daughters still in school. Public school cooking lessons (what came to be known as "home economics" classes) were the vehicle for this change. In addition to teaching different food preferences and cooking methods, home economics classes also tried to change table manners and foodshopping behavior in their efforts to "Americanize" immigrant groups. Even though older immigrant women often were resistant to these changes, food reformers usually won out with the second generation of immigrant women's daughters. Certainly generational pressure to change food behavior must have created pressures between mother and daughter in immigrant households.

Not all immigrant women were resistent to change; ethnic groups differed in their attachment to the food of the old country. Though acknowledging Italian and Jewish tenacity to old food ways, Levenstein (1988, p. 108) has suggested that housewives from some central and east European countries, such as Poland, Lithuania, Russia, and the Ukraine, seemed more amenable to change. He has suggested not only that their adaptability resulted from a devaluation of cooking as an important part of maternal role, but that these women simply came from cultures with less sophisticated food heritages not worth preserving in the new country.[6]

Regardless of ethnic background, however, working-class families were quite resistant to change in their eating habits. Cooperatives, peoples' stores, campaigns to eat more rice, and public kitchens had little real impact. Only the school lunch program, an extension of domestic science into the American public schools, had a lasting effect on the food preferences of at least second-generation immigrants. Food reformers' publicity about "the great malnutrition scare" (1907–1921) managed to convince most immigrant mothers that their children really needed the additional nutritional boost of the lunches provided in school. Fictitious claims about healthy eating also may have caused these mothers to question their own ability and judgment in determining what foods were best for their family.[7]

Food reformers also promoted a widespread belief that there was a highly significant connection between bad cooking and the urge for alcohol. Leading domestic scientists were convinced that the woman of the family had to be blamed for holding back the progress of the whole household. Homemakers were persuaded to abandon their families' old culinary traditions; they were regarded as practically superstitious in their adherence to tradition and maintenance of the home in a state of "incoherent primitiveness" (Shapiro, 1986, p. 174).

Advocacy of Artificial Feeding

One last aspect of maternal behavior was yet to be attacked by food reformers. As mentioned earlier in this chapter, middle-class women generally had social, religious, and other interests outside the home by the late 1800s. During this same time frame, working-class women increasingly were employed outside the home. Both these class influences helped create a growing need for artificial feeding for American infants. Technology was available to provide various substitutes for mother's milk. Finally, the growing medical specialty of pediatrics needed a reason for mothers to begin using their services, and individualized formulas for artificial feeding provided just such a "perk" for pediatricians struggling to create a new medical specialty. A very effective advertising campaign by producers of dried milk preparations raised questions about the ability of mothers of all classes to successfully breastfeed their infants.[8] Though native-born American women originally were most likely to adopt artificial feeding, immigrant women followed suit after being exposed to American norms and advertising. The irony of all this is that artificial feeding grew in popularity at precisely the same time public health officials first recognized that breast-fed children survived infancy with much greater frequency than did bottle-fed babies.

The growth of pediatrics in America (and prior to that in England and Germany) coincided with an increase in women reporting an inability to breastfeed their infants. These women seem to have either convinced themselves or to have been convinced by physicians that they were incapable of nursing. Recommendations that babies be nursed every two hours may have facilitated this "failure" to adequately breastfeed babies on the part of women following the dictates of pediatricians. Again we have an example of women's relationship to the food supply being manipulated for economic reasons: in this case the successful campaign to get mothers to utilize a commercial product, infant formula, instead of breastfeeding their offspring as traditional feminine roles had dictated for millenia. Furthermore, such treatment by the medical establishment and big business was likely to make women question their "natural" or innate feminine qualities which, in turn, certainly raised self-doubt about their ability to fulfill traditional feminine roles.

ACQUIESCENCE TO ADVERTISING

American food reformers latched onto an even "newer" form of nutrition at the end of World War I: vitamins. Advertisers immediately capitalized on scientists' growing awareness of the existence of vitamins in advertising for particular brands of food. Home economists also helped keep the general public concerned about the vitamins and minerals in their food.

American families became increasingly child-centered around the turn of the century, in part because abolition of child labor and enforcement of compulsory education laws extended the length of childhood for both working- and middle-class families. The end result was a growing emphasis on the mother-child relationship. Now it was even more imperative for homemakers to ensure that all members of the family receive an adequate diet including the newly discovered vitamins and minerals. Concern with nutritional adequacy was partially generated by the fact that women were increasingly relying on processed food to feed their families.

By 1913 one magazine food writer announced that "canned fruits and vegetables had so improved in quality that they were now preferable to fresh produce" (Shapiro, 1986, p. 203). At about the same time, a group of Boston food reformers declared that, at least in urban areas, "home cooking" would disappear entirely. New England Kitchen research, however, found that food tasters still preferred home-cooked food over that bought in commercial establishments (including their own). Clearly, taste considerations were being compromised to some degree for the convenience of processed foods.

The American pioneer of this latest wave of interest in nutrition, Elmer McCollum, argued in the 1920s, just as Kellogg and Post did three decades earlier, that eating "protective foods" was necessary because so many of the original nutrients had been lost in processing. Public acknowledgment of the loss in food quality, just when the American housewife truly had embraced processed food, was utilized by advertising to sell particular foodstuffs on the basis of the vitamins they contained. The blend of maternal guilt over adequacy of children's care while using possibly inferior foodstuffs to actually feed one's family was used by ingenious advertisers to assuage a mother's doubts in this dilemma.[9] A 1920s example of advertising that explicitly evoked maternal guilt was Post's campaign to sell Grape-Nuts; the ad copy asked "Are you bringing up your children properly?" since "it is possible to give children all the food they can possibly eat—and still their little bodies can be under-nourished" (Levenstein, 1988, p. 153). Increasingly, acquiescence to the judgment of so-called food experts resulted in housewives questioning their traditional foodways: their customs and the foods prepared in their own mothers' kitchens.

By the end of the 1920s, in terms of capital investment, food processing industries were larger than even such industry giants as iron, steel, and textiles. Since Americans were not willing to eat more than the abundant amount of food already available, the success of any one food commodity had to be at the expense of another food commodity. The saturated food market created great pressure on advertisers to motivate consumers to substitute one food product for another.

Betty Crocker as Friendly Anglo Ally

The "Betty Crocker" advertising phenomenon was incredibly successful in making American homemakers feel they had an ally in the kitchen. There has been no greater commercial influence on the cooking of women who came of age in the post World War II years through the 1960s. Betty's books and recipes, using lots of General Mills products, were the introduction to the kitchen for at least two generations of women. This fictional character actually was created by General Mills in the 1920s to put a "friendly face" on their responses to housewives' questions sent to the food service department. Eventually, Marjorie Husted, playing the role of Betty Crocker, provided a weekly radio program to encourage women in their cooking endeavors and to positively reinforce housewives' use of General Mills products. The fact that Betty Crocker only cooked Anglo food was to have a great homogenizing effect on what Americans ate in the twentieth century. Non-Anglo women either had to abandon their traditional taste preferences or lose the benefits of this culinary link to mainstream America.[10]

Because they were produced in a few major centers, recipes and food advice from women's magazines and the women's pages of the daily newspapers further standardized the American diet in the popular press, just as Betty Crocker's free recipes on the back of General Mills products had done. The press continued to strengthen food tastes of British origin which, after all, had always comprised the basis of middle-class eating preferences. Regional and ethnic fare increasingly was relegated to Sunday dinners, holidays, and family festivities, serving as a reminder of common origins and a common past. But there were fewer immigrants arriving in America after World War I because of more restrictive immigration laws. Much of the culinary expertise of the "old country" was being lost as second and third generation immigrant families were increasingly pressured to adopt the eating styles of the dominant American culture.[11]

Diets and Calories

American housewives were first considered the sexual and social companions of their husbands in the early decades of the twentieth century. It was inevitable, therefore, that a middle-class appreciation for slimmer bodies would follow. Women were demanding less constricting clothing so that they could move about more easily. It also became more fashionable for women to engage in milder forms of exercise outdoors. By the 1920s shorter hemlines exposed parts of the body never before revealed to the public eye. The "flapper" had a body like that of a pre-adolescent boy, a far cry from the voluptuous ideal of the nineteenth century.

"Dieting" first became a topic for discussion in the public press in the 1920s. The *Woman's Home Companion* proclaimed in 1923, "Once fat was an asset: now it's a liability, both physical and esthetic" (Levenstein, 1988, p. 166). A budding obsession with dieting and calories, at this time, resulted in a permanent reduction in meal expectations for the American middle class: a light breakfast and lunch, and a dinner of meat, potato, vegetable, and a simple dessert. This description accurately described the eating habits of most Americans for the next 60 or so years.[12] The working class, on the other hand, resisted social pressure for women to have smaller bodies for several more decades. Levenstein (1988) has observed that "while they may have admired the same skinny actors and actresses, the working class was not yet secure enough about its food supply to succumb to middle-class calorie-counting and dieting" (p. 176).

Though concern for diet and calories began in the 1920s, it wasn't until the 1950s that a dieting *industry* was born. With its inception, the average American woman began questioning her very right to food: "All the passion and imagination that domestic scientists had devoted to taming the appetite was revived and magnified in the dieting industry" (Shapiro, 1986, p. 233).

DOMESTIC SCIENCE WITHERS WOMEN'S APPETITE

It is significant that a major food reform movement swept across the country from its New England origins at precisely the same time feminism was first organizing around major political issues. Women swelled the ranks of the suffrage and temperance movements while the country as a whole obsessed over nutrients, calories, and body image. The domestic science movement gained valuable support because it represented a seemingly safer outlet for women's altruistic tendencies. If technology and science could be used to transform cooking and housework into a "professional" endeavor for middle-class housewives, perhaps they might be less interested in political and social issues outside the home. Domestic science was utilized by universities, the public school system, the government, and the food industry to help Americans "forget what they once knew about food and to content themselves with convenience, which has long been indistinguishable from progress" (Shapiro, 1986, p. 7).

Any analysis of the motivation driving the original domestic scientists also has considered the desire for personal advancement, arguing that these women were interested in gaining access to the modern world of science, technology, and rationality—a world previously reserved for men. In the end, however, this strategy gained women only second-class citizenship in that world. Domestic scientists never seemed to realize the ways they were sidetracked in their struggle for entrance into established scientific education and careers. Shapiro (1986) has insightfully articulated a parallel between the enthusiasm for domestic science nearly a century ago and current advocacy of a "post-feminist" analysis of women's role.

> Indeed, the blind faith that characterized the domestic scientists and undermined their idealism is still with us. We live in a time when feminism is considered passé, when rational assessment tells us that all the battles have been won, all the laws are in place, and the only decision women have to make is where to jump aboard. . . . They've learned to put feminism behind them, to dress for success, to play the game by men's rules, and to think like men—and they are making the domestic scientists' mistake all over again. There is still a place in every institution for women who think like men, and it's still woman's place. (pp. 9–10)

Early reformers chose domesticity as a way of getting out of the house and food as a means of transcending the body. It was never even considered, for example, that early students at the Boston Cooking School eat the meals they prepared in class, just as properly raised women were assumed not to have any real appetites. This stance denied women the normal human pleasures so readily associated with food: "By enobling the recipes over the results, and disdaining the proof of the palate, they made it possible for American cooking to accept a flood of damaging innovations for years to come" (Shapiro, 1986, p. 72). Domestic science clearly did not operate in the best interests of either the women trained in this discipline or American culinary traditions.

In addition to its devastating influence on American cooking, domestic science encouraged a negative relationship between women and food. Domestic science never intended for women to enjoy food, to develop a sense for flavors, or to acknowledge that eating could be a pleasure in itself. Rather domestic science's insistence on denial created a perfect backdrop for the development of eating issues in twentieth century American women. American women still are struggling for release from this legacy: from debilitating attitudes toward food and their own bodies.[13]

"Femininity" became fashionably associated with illness at the turn of the century when iron-deficiency anemia became widespread among adolescent girls disdaining meat in favor of white-flour products. Though identified as ill with "chlorosis" by medical professionals, the pallor of these teenage girls was considered "beautiful" in a social context. Such contradictory feedback from professionals in contrast with popular culture still occurs today as Americans worry that our adolescent girls are "too thin" while, at the same time, the culture continues to positively reinforce thinness.[14] Both examples illustrate the social reality that change in cultural embodiments of "feminine" never facilitate greater autonomy for American women.

Domestic science at the service of the all-powerful food industry had such a grip on American eating behavior that by the 1960s housewives were seen as the "assemblers" of meals, even though early food reformers knew very well, the only way to achieve real efficiency in the kitchen was to learn what to expect from basic ingredients and to know how to combine them purposefully.

The gap between real "cooking from scratch" and the reality of what people actually ate led to a two-pronged attack on dietary inadequacies during the 1960s. Exposure to the cuisines of other cultures and ethnic groups caused food writers to criticize the American diet for being too bland and homogeneous. At the same time the health food counterculture, buttressed by contemporary nutritional research, attacked the American diet as "unhealthy." These two themes certainly are, if anything, even more assertively voiced in the critical obsession with food evidenced in the late 1990s. Even though more foodstuffs are available than ever before in human history, it is ironical that as we approach the twenty-first century many Americans' diets are less healthy than at anytime in the past.

When one examines the 1990s "food mania," women's food preferences are not an important part of the picture. It still is not fashionable for a woman independently to decide what food she actually will eat rather than serve to others. This is part of the domestic science legacy which considered feminism only as a movement to afford women equality in the social and economic realms of life. The food reformers never bothered to consider women doing women's work: "What the domestic scientists really believed in was man, and what they wanted for women was progress in his name" (Shapiro, 1986, p. 236).

A WOMAN'S HOME IS HER CASTLE?

Wajcman (1991) has analyzed living space configurations as a reflection of changes in women's role over the last century. She viewed housing as an expression of women's space as gendered space. Changes in marital relationships within the twentieth century have been given physical expression through Wajcman's description of the interior design of the post–World War II home.[15]

If the second world war posed a challenge to traditional sex roles, it left little trace on the design of houses. In fact the post-war period saw a renewed advocacy of separate spheres for women and men. Housing construction during the 1950s and 1960s coincided with women being pushed back into the home to care for their husbands and children. With the rapid growth in home ownership after the war, a more home-centered lifestyle was emphasized for men as well as women. The idea of companionate marriage required the family increasingly to share activities and to cultivate intimate relationships within the comfort of the home:

> Here "good" communication, intimacy, awareness of the needs of others, shared leisure (often shared consumption) gained a prominence previously accorded to hygiene and nutrition. But . . . the continuity with Victorian middle-class domestic ideals was in many ways more profound than the discontinuities." (p. 116)

Domestic servants had finally bowed completely out of the home; consequently the illusion that meals simply arrived in the dining room, as if from nowhere, was abandoned also. Now there was less reason to have a separate kitchen and dining room; so the kitchen was enlarged and opened up to the rest of the house. This open design gave domestic work a more egalitarian appearance as other members of the family shared the space (and by implication the tasks) previously assigned to the housewife. Certainly the traditional division of labor did not change with these architectural changes; however, interior design did obscure the extent to which women continued to bear total responsibility for the care of the family. Suburban houses typically had "eat-in" kitchens, again signifying a less formal lifestyle. Open-plan kitchens enabled mothers to supervise children while cooking the meal, as children were now felt to require constant attention and companionship.

Very little privacy was provided for any family member; the home had become primarily a place for shared activities. Children's bedrooms were small, ensuring that they would spend most of their time in the larger "family room." Adults, especially women, were assumed to need even less private space in the home. Even the parents' bedroom belonged to "the Master." Women did not have a room of their own; their spatial needs were subsumed into the common space of the family. If they had a domain, it was the kitchen.

Putting women back into the home, each into her own separate housing unit, also coincided with the growing isolation of individual housewives in America. Connections with others, be they the extended family during the hard times of the depression before the war or fellow workers during stints in wartime production, had given housewives ample possibilities for socializing with other women. But the 1950s concept of "togetherness" was to undo these connections as both working- and middle-class families scrambled to get their house in the suburbs when the boys came home. It most likely was not accidental that organized dieting programs came into existence in America also during this same decade: another activity to fill the days and give shape to one's personal identity as housewife and mother.

The prototype for the modern suburban house prescribed the form of household that would inhabit it, namely the white middle-class nuclear family. As such it not only was oppressive for most women, but, with its markedly ethnocentric design, it denied the existence and needs of other forms of family.

The last third of the twentieth century has witnessed major shifts in the social position of women and in the way women have come to see themselves. American women, at least more affluent white women, have made real advances educationally, in the marketplace, and in the politics of institutional power. Paradoxically this period also has been characterized by a renewed rhetoric identifying women as soft, feminine creatures, primarily interested in home and hearth: something increasingly at odds with reality. The clinical, white plastic kitchen of post–World War II suburbia has given way to a more cozy "country kitchen" with natural wood trim and floral prints evoking the cheerful simplicity of rural life.

The kitchen has become the emotional center of the home; the relaxed, informal, symmetrical family lifestyle radiates from this hub. Power relations commonly found within the patriarchal family have been submerged beneath a popular notion of shared home responsibilities for the two-career household.

Modern home design in the last few decades of the twentieth century generally has not satisfied the housing needs of the majority of American households which, in fact, no longer are composed of nuclear families. This omission may partially explain the popularity of urban condominiums as Americans enter the twenty-first century.

Chapter 4

Moral Manipulation

The previous chapter examined the impact of changes in food distribution and preparation over the last 150 years. These changes influenced the value society bestowed on food preparers. Because women traditionally have had the responsibility for food preparation, these changes also affected women's social role in America. This chapter continues the examination of important themes, first manifested after World War II, that continue to influence Americans' relationships with food. Even the disruption radical activists created in the food supply, along with every other aspect of American society, during the decades of the 1960s and1970s ultimately was assimilated by big business and used to sell more goods.

COUNTERCULTURE CREATES COUNTERCUISINE

Warren Belasco (1989) has documented the 1960s new-left creation of "countercuisine" in his delightful volume, *Appetite for Change*. Countercuisine was conceived to be a weapon for fighting the establishment. The logic of the new left had always insisted that the personal was political. What could be more personal than food? And what could be more political than challenging agribusiness, America's largest and most environmentally troublesome industry.

Anthropologists have long understood that what an individual eats in many ways defines that individual. Every society, in fact, derives its cuisine out of a much wider range of options: "The human race as a whole is omnivorous, but individual societies are picky" (Belasco, 1989, p. 44). A basic cultural process narrows the range of choices in the course of evolving a cuisine unique to that particular culture. Members of a particular society collectively decide over time what is considered good to eat, and what foods should be avoided. A cuisine, therefore, is a categorization that helps society's members define themselves. This sort of societal self-definition establishes who are insiders or outsiders to that group. Like language, a cuisine is a medium by which a society establishes its special identity.

Countercuisine, therefore, was a set of food reforms defining the counterculture; it was comprised of three elements that collectively established a coherent set of dietary beliefs and practices. The consumerist component offered survivalist advice and suggested what to avoid, especially processed, "plastic" food. While radical consumerism was largely negative, the second, therapeutic component suggested ways to make food more fun through a delight in improvisation, craftmanship, and ethnic and regional cooking. Addressing issues of food production and distribution, the third element was the organic paradigm, which posited a radically decentralized infrastructure consisting of communal farms, cooperative groceries, and hip restaurants.

Given the importance of cuisine in establishing group identity, it was not suprising that a countercuisine helped define the1960s social movement known as the counterculture. Not only did new eating patterns encourage consumption of foods with which the individual was very likely previously unfamiliar, such as kiwi and other fruits from faraway countries or, perhaps, little-known indigenous edibles like arugula and lamb's ear. But the countercuisine also combined foodstuffs in unique and imaginative ways—for example, peanut-butter-and-banana sandwiches. In the counterculture food was a medium of communication and a form of subversion, much like music, sex and drugs.

It is important to remember that for most Americans the prevailing cuisine prior to this time was a meat-and-potatoes Anglo cuisine that had been reinforced by the marketing and advertising arms of the giant food processors for decades. It did not take much effort, therefore, to create what generally were perceived to be radically new and different dishes. Adapting dishes from other already existing cuisines was another quick way for a hippie cook to appear unique in her or his food preparations since America had little national recognition of ethnic or other "foreign" dishes at this time. A dish containing both black beans and rice, for example, would have seemed radical in the prevailing American culture of the late 1960s unless one were already familiar with, say, the "rice and peas" basic to Caribbean cuisines.

The concept of the "oppositional identity" (Belasco, 1989) is important for understanding why hippies romantically and enthusiastically embraced seeming paradoxes and even had fun while doing so. The counterculture went natural not only for survival but also for fulfillment. Dietary primitivism would purge and protect you, but it would also make you well, perhaps even happy. Food paradoxes originally established in the 1970s are still being debated in 1990s culinary circles: natural foods were safer *and* tastier; wild greens were hardscrabble staples *and* gourmet treats; ethnic foods were cheap *and* rich; vegetarianism seemed ecologically *and* spiritually sound; exercise and dieting made you a better street fighter *and* lover.

The countercuisine, therefore, had therapeutic, survivalist, and organic (especially in fighting the contamination and pollution of modern life) themes. One therapeutic thread of the countercuisine involved an "eating the other" dynamic (Belasco, 1989) since hippies believed that a voracious exploration of other regional and ethnic cuisines could help one find oneself. In other words, one could perhaps acquire new beliefs or identity simply by trying out a new way of eating. This tendency to define one's self through consumption of the foods of other cultures and ethnic groups re-emerged in the "foodie" phenomenon of the 1980s and is discussed later in this chapter. There is even an oppositional tension embedded in the "eating the other" concept. Consumption was desirable in the counterculture but only if it was not "piggy," meaning the indiscriminate and excessive intake of any food. After all, such gross and excessive behavior was something cops and other members of the establishment did.

Another therapeutic thread of the countercuisine was spun from the counterculture notion that it was spiritually most desirable to "live lightly on the earth." This belief capsulized the determination to live both hedonistically and ecologically, to be both effervescent and ascetic, bohemian and peasant.[1] The notion of "lite" as it was marketed by the food industry over the next few decades serves as a good example of the processors' reduction of the original, multifaceted notion of "living lightly" into a single-minded advertising theme: by staying light in weight, one could appear young forever. By the close of the 1970s, the food industry's oversimplification of a spiritual, ecological, and behavioral ideal had, in reality, fueled a cultural preoccupation with weight and a demand for smaller bodies for all Americans.

BIG BUSINESS MANIPULATES THE COUNTERCUISINE

Initially, the food giants and their handmaidens in government and the academe argued that life before processing was barely worth living. Removing additives might mean the return of rickets, pellagra, and scurvy; eliminating preservatives would encourage botulism, salmonella, and dysentery. By eating organically, the American diet would be no different than that of any third world country. When it became apparent, however, that countercuisine was not going to disappear even with such scare tactics, the food industry co-opted the countercuisine use of terms such as "natural foods" and "lite foods," playing with consumers' fears that their food had too little nutritional value. Examples of big business' manipulation of the food supply illustrate yet another way in which the consumer remained divorced from meaningful connections with the food she prepared and ate with her family.

In the countercuisine, "natural" had three dimensions: content (more nutrients, no chemicals); time (older); and a state of mind (nonrational, romantic, improvisational). The last component was the hardest to mainstream for it defied standardization.

The food industry first did what it knows best; it added back what had already been removed in food processing, a technique Belasco (1989) has referred to as "nutrification." Rather than changing basic production modes to alleviate the necessity for nutrification, manufacturers simply added back what they had taken out. They also raised the price for the resultant "new," "improved," "natural" product. It actually was easier for the consumer to take another pill or fortified flake than to consider fighting old nutritional habits.

It could be argued that it would have made more sense to eat fresh produce to get those vitamins and minerals and, in truth, Americans were eating more fresh produce. For many Americans, however, eating a vegetable was like taking a pill: a chore performed for the sake of nutrition, not taste. Consumer resistance to fresh produce was adamant until the advent of better educated, more affluent, food-conscious yuppies of the 1980s when almost 50 percent of higher income people reported eating more fresh produce (Belasco, 1989, p. 219).

Even the new salad bars did not protect consumers from additives and other chemicals used to grow fruits and vegetables: "Food engineers who were otherwise wary of healthy foods became boyishly enthusiastic when they pondered ways to keep tomatoes and strawberries 'fresh' by hidden technologies such as irradiation and genetic engineering" (Belasco, 1989, p. 219).

Like fortification, therefore, the provision of fresh produce offered the food industry a relatively congenial and profitable way to present a healthy front, gain upscale customers, and deflect attention from more troublesome concerns. Food processors found that bullying growers into signing with a major brand conglomerate allowed them to recoup losses in the canning industry. They also were able to finalize their control over food production in America and, ultimately, the world.

The problem of nutritional content in the public's perception of "natural" actually was solved by adding more chemicals to the grains, fruit, and produce Americans were eating. Of course the consumer usually was unaware of these additives. In reality the content of mass-marketed natural foods could be as vague as the word itself. The countercuisine's use of "natural" was both negative (no chemicals, little processing) and positive (more vitality). The negative side was tougher for processors to co-opt. By altering production, manufacturers sometimes did cut questionable ingredients while maintaining high food value; but few could eliminate *all* questionable ingredients, especially the salt and sweeteners added to compensate for the taste lost through processing.

Mainstreaming the time component of "natural" was easier for it was relatively more finite: "Many Americans appeared to date the decline of western civilization from the arrival of the automobile, electric light bulb, and skyscraper. Conversely, a product seemed healthier, more natural, if it somehow suggested life before 1910" (Belasco, 1989, p. 221). Individualizing chain restaurants' decor, using earth tones in the packaging of supermarket foods, and emphasizing historic associations of the food manufacturer were some of the techniques used to convey a sense of connection with the past, when food was pure and simple.

Retailing natural foods over time illustrated a "convergence dynamic" (Belasco, 1989) whereby major supermarket chains integrated "natural" features while independent sellers of natural foods adopted mainstream practices; this was especially apparent in the independents' tendency to move up the food chain away from minimally processed commodities toward high-profit dietary supplements, cosmetics, snacks, and labor-saving packaged products. For one-stop convenience, some natural food chains actually relocated to malls and achieved supermarket size.

The food industry capitalized on the counterculture notion of "living lightly" in its highly successful campaign to market "lite" foods. The mainstream notion of "lite," however, focused primarily on the more tangible goal of reducing fat and calories to maintain youthful slimness. Beginning in the 1970s marketers used "lite" to replace "diet" as they repositioned products to appeal to both sides of the consumer's struggle to have both taste *and* health, defined as thinner. An ability to overcome basic contradictions was most appealing to food industry sectors struggling with flagrant tension between healthy *and* tasty or healthy *and* quick. For example, a choice between alcoholic beverages *and* soft drinks or homecooking *and* fast food.

Though "lite" foods seemed to possess a more defined and tangible benefit than "natural" foods, their actual 1980s legal definition was even more vague, another advantage to manufacturers. Since regulators did not consider "lite" a nutritional claim until the 1990s, product labels did not have to substantiate such claims. Frequently cheaper to make, "lite" products still commanded equivalent or even premium prices. And food manufacturers knew from demographic research that the typical "lite" customer (read "yuppie") clearly could afford the higher prices.

Big business also co-opted the early 1970s counterculture in its use of the nudity associated with communes as a sexy way to sell products. Belasco (1989) has analyzed *Playboy* magazine's photo spreads of nude models in hip communal settings. Compared to real communal settings, however, these models were seductively curvy yet slim, sort of "hip but not hippy."[2]

A renewed emphasis on body image as a barometer of self-worth was a second misinterpretation of advertisers' use of nudity to sell food products. In the mainstream, being thin as a hippie was seen as one way to stay young and beautiful; this was a misinterpretation of the "live lightly" doctrine, even when the lean body resulted from intentional modifications of diet for moral or ethical reasons. Frances Moore Lappe (1971), for example, tried to talk about the world food crisis on talk shows only to find her hosts discussing *Diet for a Small Planet* as a weight-loss manual. The counterculture actually had struggled for freedom from social restraint, including the social demand that females maintain small bodies. Throughout the 1970s, advertising systematically reduced the likelihood that a woman could feel good about her body regardless of size; representations of the counterculture in 1970s product advertising simply renewed the old refrain that "smaller is better."

A very different sort of manipulation, one specifically targeting women this time, occurred when the food industry tried to take credit for the social gains resulting from the counterculture's American "revolution." In this case individual consumers were not targeted for manipulation; rather an attempt was made to manipulate women as a whole.

Advertisers actually asserted that the 1960s second wave of feminism was caused by modern appliances and convenience foods. They argued that women increasingly were free to enter the workforce because new convenience foods and technology made it possible for women workers to spend less time in the kitchen and more time out of the home augmenting their family's income. Even the well-respected nutritionist, Jean Mayer, suggested that "the additives in convenience foods were a precondition for the women's liberation movement" (Belasco, 1989, p. 124) since additives eliminated the need for the time-consuming preparation of fresh food for the family each day of the week.

Food processors were ingenious in their attempts to convince the American public that *they* were responsible for creating the affluent prerequisites for rebellion. By freeing up women in the kitchen, it was now possible for these same wives and mothers to competitively enter the marketplace. To some degree this was true, but what was really novel in their argument was "the assertion that the revived drive for women's rights in the late 1960s was caused by the blender, toaster oven, and instant pudding mix" (Belasco, 1989, p. 124). Ironically, as recently as the 1950s, food advertisements and articles in women's magazines actually had encouraged just the opposite: convenience goods really helped to preserve feminine dependency and domesticity.

Minimizing or ignoring women's considerable efforts to further feminist goals in education and career opportunities during the second wave of feminism was the most egregious manipulation of all. Not only were women displaced from the kitchen, the place where they previously felt pride in their accomplishments, but now the food industry's celebration of food processors and such as a measure of women's social progress smacked of the very same tactics that were used to put domestic scientists in their place!

BIG BROTHER MANIPULATED BY BIG BUSINESS

The Food and Drug Administration (FDA) was created in 1906 by a progressive federal government interested in efficiency and reform. Historians remind us, however, that the relationship between the FDA and the industries it regulated was cozy from the first. Many exposés over the years have implicated the FDA in compromises of hygiene and quality for various foodstuffs; so the general public is somewhat knowledgeable of such complicity. What might not be so well known is the suggestion of some historians (Belasco, 1989) that this agency sometimes may have set regulations for petty or financial reasons instead of acting on the basis of their mandate from Congress.

A good example of differential treatment involved the FDA's handling of established, large-scale food manufacturers, the ones who had co-opted the countercuisine, in their move to market so-called healthy foods. A laissez-faire policy prevailed and the FDA did not interfere with the big food processors. The FDA has behaved very differently, however, in its ongoing crusade to curb and control the health food industry over the last several decades.

The FDA's crackdown on the health food industry over the last several decades illustrates the inconsistent, authoritarian decisions sometimes made by this bureacracy. An FDA attempt to limit vitamin dosages in 1974 resulted in enormous protest over what was perceived as an attempt on the part of the federal government to hinder self-medication by ordinary citizens. After being flooded with protests from citizens opposing the vitamin decision, Congress voted to limit the FDA's authority. A similar attempt and resulting outcry occurred in the 1990s. The long battle among food producers over construction and inclusion in the "good nutrition pyramid" during the same decade illustrates how FDA policy has changed as a result of influence from outside business interests.

In the 1990s the general public finally became aware of the need to eat less meat and more fish and vegetable proteins; their knowledge of better nutrition resulted from publicity funded by the government. Yet the American government, at the same time, continued to offer farmers reduced fees on public grazing lands; it also continued to pay for the feed used to raise cattle, hogs, and poultry. These indirect payments helped keep meat and dairy prices low. In addition, the government continued a so-called checkoff program in which a portion of the profit from every sale of a head of cattle or a hundred-weight of milk went into a kitty that financed the government-run campaign of generic ads. The fund was not insubstantial; in 1995 it amounted to more than $300 million for beef and dairy alone. In reality this program actually provided free advertising for meat and dairy products. A final perk for these industries' sales involved the school lunch program where 20 percent of the food came from government surplus, mostly cheese and butter (Drexler, 1996). The government's heavy favoritism toward meat and dairy industries has simply encouraged American citizens to keep eating the less healthy diet of their parents' generation: the one that defied the government's own latest nutritional advice.[3]

FEMINISTS DISCOVER ECOLOGY

It was inevitable that the 1960s second wave of feminism would interface with the counterculture. Both movements had their roots in the civil rights and antiwar movements. And many women were involved in both the new left and feminist activities. When the counterculture went "back to nature," part of that theme signaled a growing appreciation of one's natural environment or "ecology," a newly popular field of study. Though they were busy challenging road blocks in an expansion of women's role in American culture, 1960s feminists also were experiencing a growing appreciation of nature and the tasks involved in their so-called natural role, such as cooking, baking, gardening, and working with fibers.

Will It Be Tarzan and Jane or Xena?

Tension was growing in the counterculture over men's use of women for "free love" and other grunt work. Many feminists resented the male counterculture view of women as still being defined by their biology (reproductive and sexual roles) even within the movement. Robin Morgan captured the female paradox of participation in both movements in her dismissal of male ecologists "tripping off women as earth-mother or frontier chicks" but understanding, at the same time, that women's bodies were "unavoidably aware of the locked-in relationship between humans and their biosphere—the earth, the tides, the atmosphere, the moon" (Belasco, 1989, p. 35).

Several points about what was then referred to as "feminist ecology" are relevant to any discussion of the convolution of food, feminism, and fat during this time frame. The issue of "pigs" is a case in point. "Pigs" was the term applied to policemen by the counterculture. But this term was a metaphor for more than just law enforcement officers. A pig was related to fat, which itself was a longstanding metaphor for bourgeois affluence, softness, and corruption. So when the underground press advised readers not to "pig out," food writers were more concerned for readers' minds than waistlines. This rhetorical battle against pigs and fat had special resonance for women since they generally wrote and certainly read underground consumer columns. Negative imagery about body fat certainly continued after the counterculture finally faded into the very categories they protested so mightily in their youth. The twentieth century has been unique in its constantly intensified cultural articulation of negative imagery concerning body fat.

The more radical segment of the broad based, popular ecology movement evolved as the decade progressed into what is often referred to today as ecofeminism. This specialized segment of the more broad-based environmental movement focused on the connection between violence against women and animals and the destruction of the very earth itself.[4] For example, feminist survivalists (forerunners to later ecofeminists?) emphasized physical fitness via practice of some form of self-defense in the Berkeley women's paper, *It Ain't Me Babe*. Here it was theorized that the ability to physically defend oneself would expand a woman's social role possibilities and, at the same time, release women from their former reliance on men for self-definition and protection.

The struggle for self-control through self-defense also led to a generalized attack on the health delivery systems, felt to have been created by the establishment for "male-feasance." Male doctors, druggists, government health officials, academic experts, grocers, and food processors all were accused of exploiting or, at best, ignoring women's needs.[5]

Healthy eating also was promoted as a feminist priority. Advice about dieting was ambivalent, however, since some feminists viewed dieting as a means of conforming to male images of beauty, while others felt compulsive eating caused women often to feel helpless and powerless.[6] Feminists wrote that consciousness raising would make women more comfortable with their bodies. Once they felt more comfortable, women also would be able to control other aspects of their lives.

This 1960s refrain sounded the prelude for a popular feminist belief at the close of the century (Chernin, 1981, 1985; Orbach, 1978; Roth, 1982, 1984, 1991) that an emphasis on controlling one's appetite might occur when a woman experiences a lack of personal control over other aspects of her life. Similar interpretations also can be found in literature promoting several weight control programs popular throughout America at the turn of the twenty-first century.

Themes of self-control and self-defense even ran through feminist discussions of conventional cooking. In an article titled "Nothin' Says Lovin' Like Somethin' from the Oven," *off our backs* writer Norma Allen Lesser accused cookbook writers of subtle seduction. Cookbooks promising easy-to-make meals with "gourmet appeal" and "foreign flair" were felt to exploit housewives' boredom, anxiety, and their need for creative accomplishment. Belasco's observation that "once again, a product is being subsidized by appealing to the insecurities of women" (1989, p. 36) parallels the advertising strategies of the giant food processors of the late nineteenth century (Levenstein, 1988). The exploitation of women for the purpose of selling products still existed one hundred years after processed foods were first mass-marketed in America.

Since women still did most of the cooking, feminists debated whether the priority of craft over convenience was sexist. Women experienced the proverbial horns of a dilemma over cooking. Rejecting convenience products, on the one hand, reasserted female competence and control, much as the revival of midwifery, witchcraft, and other forms of folk self-health became a feminist defense against modern medical patriarchy. However, cooking without packaged aids and appliances was more work, especially if you were not used to going primitive.

There was, moreover, a regressive tone in some counterculture cookbooks extolling premodern housewifery. Some of the time-consuming culinary work could seem boring or tedious, especially for working women who were too rushed to appreciate household craftsmanship. If the amount of work demanded in the kitchen required a woman to reexamine her commitment to a career in business or some profession, then so be it. This counterculture attitude was an uncomfortably conservative critique of the two-career family model which was just beginning its ascendency into mainstream middle-class life.

Communal living was one tentative solution to the restrictions of conventional lifestyles during the 1960s and 1970s. Being a "health food nut," for example, did confer identity but could be a lonely undertaking in the family dining room or school cafeteria; but with communal life, it was felt that one could go beyond personal protest to build a cohesive model community.[7]

One first-hand observer concluded that the garden and the kitchen were the enterprises that best brought people together. This statement could be interpreted to suggest that, even in communes, it still was women's responsibility to nurture and facilitate social interactions. But even these soothing spaces apparently were not enough to maintain a sense of community when, down deep, its members did not really like each other anymore. Perhaps communes were too innocent or prepubescent to survive over time.

Particularly disheartening were the experiences of communal women who learned the hard way how sexist the 1960s organic tribe could be. Although some in the new left and the counterculture did care about developing new gender roles, free sex was, no doubt, more important to many men. As one Berkeley communard put it, for many men the best way to "smash monogamy" was to sleep with several women (Belasco, 1989). This sort of thinking propelled many communal women into the feminist movement by the end of the decade. For all too many hip women, the escape to the country meant further isolation and a return to the drudgery of the nineteenth-century homestead; now however, frontier chicks / earth mothers had the added burden of having to be sexually accessible as well.

Frances Moore Lappe as Ecofeminist Role Model

Women's passionate involvement in the early battle against pollution during the late 1960s foreshadowed their future involvement and frequent leadership in environmental groups. Such groups quickly caught on, emerging as the left's primary vehicle for outrage and hope, edging aside civil rights, the antiwar movement, and revolutionary socialism. Environmentalism now was being referred to as ecology and continued to attract women to its ranks. Women's focus, however, tended to be global, reflecting a sensitivity to the health of the planet; women's concern was not just with the pollution of the food supply, as reflected in the advocacy of vegetarian and macrobiotic food philosophies, for example, but quickly generalized into concern over pollution and shortages in the global food supply.

Frances Moore Lappe has stood as a lasting example of the metamorphosis of 1960s antiwar protesters into 1970s environmental activists. Discouraged by the antiwar movement and her futile social work job, Lappe turned to ecology in 1969. As her friends began to go natural, Lappe started playing with all sorts of peculiar foods like tofu, mung beans, bulgur, soy grits, and buckwheat groats.[8] New flavors restored a sense of intentionality and contact to what previously had seemed to be humdrum chores. As new food combinations became more attractive, shopping for food and cooking were no longer unconscious and boring, but now a real adventure. As culinary barriers broke down, so did other assumptions; Lappe began to question conventional wisdom about nutrition and world hunger.

Lappe pursued her research into the agricultural library at Berkeley and found a theoretical underpinning for her own random culinary experiments in the theory of protein complimentarity. She found that it really was possible to meet daily protein needs without resorting to ecologically wasteful meat or morally reprehensible dairy products.

Chapter 5

The More We Change, the More We Stay the Same

The 1960s witnessed the birth of two seemingly contradictory culinary trends in America: a desire for more sophisticated "gourmet" food that was fueled by both an increase in foreign tourist travel and the immediate popularity of Julia Child's "French Chef" cooking program on public television. However, at the same time, a widespread and sustained criticism of the American diet began, instigated by the counterculture and constantly reinforced by new findings in nutritional research. Both these themes still are very much in evidence at the turn of the century.

FOOD AS A STATUS SYMBOL

Americans have been eating out with ever-greater frequency; by the late 1990s, nearly half of the money spent on food was spent on food consumed outside the home. Unless a serious economic downturn occurs, that trend is expected to continue into the twenty-first century. Entertaining guests at home with food, and conspicuous eating have become central clauses in the idiom of affluence during the last two decades of the twentieth century. To some degree, the greater amounts of money spent on food both within and outside the home has been rationalized by a belief that consumption of quality or gourmet food is a prerequisite for social success. Mintz (1996) has argued, however, that what is eaten out usually is not gourmet food and certainly does not constitute a cuisine. He believes that, when Americans eat out, they simply eat the foods they like best: hamburgers, fried chicken, pizza, and baked potatoes with lots of toppings.[1]

Regardless of what the average American eats, gourmet cuisine has firmly embedded itself into American eating styles since the 1960s. Originally the term "gourmet" was synonymous with French cuisine in the minds of most Americans; but with exposure to other cultures' cuisines in the ever-shrinking world of the late twentieth century, Americans have become familiar with the food of at least a few other cuisines: Mexican and Thai, in addition to the ubiquitous Chinese takeout and, maybe, special meals in French or Italian restaurants. In their minds, anything "foreign" constitutes gourmet food. The two terms still are used interchangeably by the average American.

Probably the most important factor in the growing popularity of authentic gourmet food in America has been the increasing availability of high quality, often esoteric, ingredients: the prerequisite for genuine gourmet preparations. A great increase in the ownership of appliances and the paraphernalia required to prepare gourmet meals at home also has helped this trend; the food processor, for example, became standard equipment in most American kitchens during the 1980s.[2]

During the latter part of the twentieth century, the great popularity of cooking instruction—be it on television, in the print and video media, or classes at the local adult learning center—indicates a desire to engage gourmet cuisine on a personal, experiential basis. Individuals utilizing such instruction perhaps truly enjoy learning new cooking techniques. But all too often, food consumed or served to guests has been used as a convenient way to present one's socioeconomic class and lifestyle preferences.[3]

Yuppie Excess

After World War II ended and the boys came home to their wives and sweethearts, the ensuing families mass migrated to the newly developed suburbs. In her entertaining account of the 1980s rise and fall of the yuppies, Ehrenreich (1989) has stated that yuppies actually were the children of first generation suburbanites. Yuppies used personal consumption to express taste and level of affluence since it was unlikely they actually would acquire the homes and other financial assets of their parents' generation.

In Ehrenreich's view, it all began with a conformist, male-dominated culture in post–World War II America. This generation assumed that every male "breadwinner" deserved a "family wage" sufficient to support a wife and several children at home in a suburban cottage made accessible by exceptionally cheap energy, transportation, credit, and real estate. Although many Americans, especially minorities, remained excluded from the dream, business and political leaders generally pitched this vision as the route to a capitalist utopia.

During the expansionist years of the 1950s and 1960s, a middle-class lifestyle of the sort idealized in the TV sitcoms of the period seemed within the reach of most Americans. Making up for the deprivations of the 1930s and 1940s, American consumers kept marketers busy as they purchased the basic accoutrements of that lifestyle: a home and furnishings, a family car, television, kitchen appliances, the latest convenience foods, an occasional dinner at a family restaurant, and a summer vacation. As the economy slowed down and inflation heated up in the 1970s, it increasingly took two jobs to achieve the middle-class lifestyle once supplied by a single wage earner.

By the late 1970s the middle class had seriously shrunk in size as the gap widened between the two cultures emerging out of the former middle class. The resultant two-tier society produced what has been called the upscale and downscale cultures (Belasco, 1989). The upscale group, referred to as yuppies during the 1980s, set patterns for use of disposable income that actually persisted throughout the remainder of the century. Consumption of food, both within the home and dining out, became a status symbol. Concern about health and fitness, especially as the boomers have begun hitting age fifty, is reflected in their preference for so-called healthy, low-fat foods. These food preferences at the end of the century furthermore differentiate upscale eaters from members of lower social classes who persist in eating the same meat-and-fat-saturated diet that their parents ate a generation before.

Lumping It All Together

While ethnographers might wince at a synonymous discussion of ethnic, gourmet, and regional foods, differences among these foods actually got blurred during the 1970s and 1980s. In addition to America's love affair with foreign, especially French, cuisine, regional foods were used by self-identified foodies of both the elitist and populist camps to convey the exclusivity of their quests (Belasco, 1989). Elitists were fascinated by such historically indigenous and currently endangered American fare as buffalo steaks, morel mushrooms, wild rice, and fiddlehead ferns. Populists, on the other hand, were more likely to track down historical clambakes, "authentic" southern barbecue, and funky dishes like Philadelphia cheese steaks and Buffalo chicken wings.

In the end, though, both camps interested in regional foods really were reacting to modern aspects of the food supply. It was relatively easy to avoid mass marketing elite ingredients since they were just too delicate and scarce for large-scale distribution. The downscale funky "character" of the populist camp, however, continued to be marketed via regional food newsletters (with short membership lists) and specialty mail order catalogs and magazines.

In the otherwise bland, highly rationalized and bureaucratic environment of the last decades of the twentieth century, authentic foods suggest a smattering of spice, irregularity, and eccentricity; of real people and places; of old-fashioned honest labor and honest materials; in other words, an appearance of food lower down the food chain than it actually is. Even with their excesses, the end-of-the-century foodies have contributed a special awareness of food politics to the ongoing debate: is there is a connection between a healthy diet and the health of the planet?

IS OUR FOOD HEALTHY AND SAFE?

Concern about the food we eat has existed at least since the advent of food processing in the nineteenth century; however, anxiety around this old question grew exponentially after the 1960s counterculture made food safety a public issue. Research on food contaminants by early food activists like Lappe spurred organizational efforts to educate the general public about food dangers. Food co-ops provided another effective means for disseminating consumer information. Americans in general became more critical of the food they ate as a result of counterculture concerns about the nation's food supply. Perhaps it is more accurate to say that consumers first articulated a *desire* for healthier foods in the 1960s; whether or not the nation's eating patterns actually changed during this period is very much a matter for debate.

Americans have always had ambivalence about the necessity for healthy eating. Since the counterculture first focused attention on healthy food, people have felt that what is "good for you" could not also taste good. According to one nutritional anthropologist, many people distinguish "food" from "nutrition." "Food" is what "tastes good" while "nutrition" is what's "good for you." You get "food" in supermarkets and restaurants, and "nutrients" in drugstores, usually in vitamin pills. You "eat" food throughout the day, while you "take" nutrients once a day to compensate for dietary sins (Belasco, 1989, p. 197).

By the 1990s, twenty-two cents of every dollar spent on a meal at home went to the producer. The rest was consumed by processing, packaging, distribution, retail, transportation, labor, storage, and advertising (Drexler, 1996). Because of this arrangement, whole foods that are prepared by the individual consumer generally cost much less than processed foods. Processed foods have always been where the profits lay; that is why food advertising budgets always have been greater for processed foods than for raw foods. The general public actually has had little exposure to media advertising for whole foods while, at the same time, a great deal of exposure to media food advertising has encouraged them to purchase processed foods. There simply is more corporate profit in unhealthful food than in healthful food.[4]

Even the media's treatment of health issues during the 1980s compounded skepticism about what is "good for you." As the food scare stories kept appearing, it was easy to believe that everything caused cancer, so why bother at all? If the food establishment had deliberately set out to confuse people, it could not have done a better job. Although confusion about what *is* healthy food was voiced throughout the population, those least familiar with the style and inconclusivity of scientific debate were even more likely to adopt a nihilistic attitude toward food safety issues.

Perhaps longstanding gender, ethnic, and class patterns also may have retarded food-related health reforms during the 1980s. On the whole, men seemed less interested in health reform. This gender difference may have been the result of nutritional science and other diet-related professions having been feminized in the late nineteenth century, thereby relegating these professions to a marginal status in patriarchal culture.

In many working-class and ethnic subcultures, women subordinated their own nutritional concerns to the nutritional preferences of husband and children, healthy or otherwise; one example common in many ethnic groups is the act of serving a rich food, however "unhealthy," as a form of gift giving.[5]

Region, too, was a variable. During the 1980s, surveys consistently reported that people on the coasts and in larger metropolitan areas were somewhat more health conscious than those in the middle and southern states, smaller cities, and rural areas. Southerners were poorer and less educated than people in other areas. They also knew least about good nutrition and, conversely, were the most avid consumers of fast food, a tendency found in rural areas throughout the country. The meat culture was most firmly embedded in the rural midwest and mountain states, areas economically dependent on growing feed and raising lifestock.

The late 1990s have found America awash in media headlines about dangers from a contaminated food supply even in this country of abundance and governmental regulations. The addition of antibiotics, steroids, and other hormones to the meat and dairy supply in America has been greatly publicized and criticized, especially after the 1996 outbreak of mad cow disease in England. But bioengineering of specific vegetables through a manipulation of DNA has caused even vegetarians concern over what *else* exists in the produce they eat (Yamada, 1995). The finding that a 50 percent average drop in human sperm counts has occurred around the world over the last two generations has provided an impetus for entire books to be written about the possibility of hormone-disrupting chemicals persisting in the physical environment decades after DDT had been outlawed in the western world (Colborn, Dumanoski and Myers, 1997). Even the very seeds used to grow crops are being scrutinized for genetic manipulation as one means to diversify through excessive use of F-1 hybrids (Pollan, 1994). Ethnobotanists already had observed that use of the F-1 hybrids required growers to buy new seed each growing season while concurrently reducing genetic diversity in general. Perhaps in part because of public concern over contaminants such as these, President Clinton signed a "peace of mind act" into law in 1996; it has established uniform standards to limit chemical residues in food (Clinton signs bill, 1996). Because children are known to be especially sensitive to residues in food, the Food Quality Protection Act allows a cancer risk level of only one in a million as a lifetime exposure for both raw and processed foods. Ironically, the President's speech at the signing of this very bill included his call for "new steps using cutting-edge technology to keep our food safe," including irradiation (Kennedy, 1998, p. 7). Though irradiation had already been approved for spices, fruits, vegetables, and poultry, the FDA only approved irradiation of red meat in 1997, the same year a CBS News poll found that 77 percent of Americans "don't want to eat irradiated food" (Kennedy, 1998, p. 7).

A similar irony manifested itself in the 1998 USDA proposal to lower the minimum standards set in the 1990 Organic Foods Production Act (Goodman, 1998.) These proposals would allow lettuce fertilized with sewage sludge, genetically engineered animals destined for human consumption, and irradiated produce all to carry the label "organic." The American public's subsequent outrage was predictable given the results of the CBS poll that same year. If the USDA proposals become law, "organic will have lost any meaning. The 'O' in the O-word will stand for Zero" (p. A27).

COMFORT FOOD WILL MAKE EVERYTHING OKAY

An "anti-health" trend may have occurred in the mid-1980s, as some food observers reported a turnabout in efforts to seek out healthy food. The same generation that had advocated natural, lite, maybe even organic food during its formative years began to crave the "square" food of its youth. On the surface the anti-health trend seemed to confirm what many believed or hoped; that history was basically cyclical, that sooner or later just about everything that "goes around, comes around."[6]

Seeking their own roots in the 1980s, "neosquares" turned inward and autobiographical, to the foods they were most nostalgic for as reflections of their youth: foods such as tuna noodle casserole or Spam sandwiches.[7] This retro vision of the food eaten when young often involved a deconstruction of the actual reality of youthful mealtimes. Remembering the 1980s culinary craze for American food, one observer has commented that what's really American about American cooking is change; we don't cook the way our mothers did, and neither did our mothers. And with change always comes another opportunity for big business to make more money selling Americans what they, at that moment, think they want to eat.

A parallel existed between retro cuisine in the 1980s and earlier hippie use of food as a panacea in the 1960s. Observing how difficult it was for hip communards to sustain their guise of childlike innocence amidst the troubles of the late 1960s, Ray Mungo wrote that it was awfully difficult to be nine once you would never see nineteen again. Political and biological realities had a way of catching up. The war, the environment, the economy all had a way of making their demands felt, even in Vermont. Chic meat loafers of the 1980s had similar concerns, but now the apocalypse was fifteen years closer: "The cracks were too wide to be patched by extralarge portions of meat and potatoes" (Belasco, 1989, p. 242).

FOOD AND EATING AS A MORALITY PLAY

Many late twentieth century Americans have manifested a compulsive concern for the way their body is seen and assessed, which, in turn, has translated into aggravated attitudes and feelings about food. Anthropological research into the culinary meaning of this exaggerated concern has suggested that such individuals really believe self control is measured by one's ability to control, manage, and discipline one's body. From this perspective, every act of eating is a test of will. Since eating is morally colored, it is no suprise that half of the American people, 90 percent of all American women, consider themselves to be dieting at any one time in the late 1990s.[8]

The previous chapter introduced two major criticisms of American diet that were first articulated in the 1960s: our cuisine was not sophisticated enough and, at the same time, our food was not healthy enough. Certainly these forces, if anything, exist even more powerfully at the end of the century. Consider the enormous popularity of Julia Child in this country over the last four decades as proof of the former. But a secondary result of this American love affair with French food has been a growing appreciation of food as a means of self-definition and a measure of self-worth. The fusion of food and identity, in turn, has triggered great concern about what people eat. Once this new self-consciousness about food took hold, the rest was only a matter of time: "Food . . . has become eroticized, politicized, fetishized, and invested with symbolism and moral power as never before in American society" (Iggers, 1993, p. 54).

Is Eating the Oldest Sin?

Group dieting centers were established at a frantic pace in 1950s America. That decade gave birth to Overeaters' Anonymous with its extreme notion that overeating was a compulsion that had to be controlled over a lifetime via severe dietary rules and restrictions. Weight Watchers arrived a few years later and precipitated look-alikes as the decade grew older. Several of the group dieting programs shared a trend toward public confessionals, complete with guilt and shame, regarding weight and eating problems. Large numbers of individuals, especially women, continued to be attracted to this group format for the remainder of the century (Seid, 1989).

A variation of the group dieting centers' refrain could be heard among Americans in general during the last two decades of the twentieth century. Iggers, for example, remarked in 1993 that "if it is remarkable how riddled with guilt our relationship with food has become, it is even more noteworthy how much our morality has become centered on food" (p. 56). The previously vast realm of guilt-provoking areas in life has shrunk to a "beleaguered enclave" dominated by our morally problematic interaction with food: "At the heart of this new food guilt is a migration of both our eroticism and our moral focus from our groins to our guts"(p. 58). Perhaps the essence of personal identity has shifted from how one is connected to the social world, typical of Victorian times when sex was loaded with expectation and responsibility, to a more modern world in which individualism and privacy are valued greatly, one in which an individual is defined by what is consumed rather than by connections.

Food consumption consistently has had negative meaning throughout the twentieth century; however, the specific negative message given has changed over time. For an earlier-twentieth-century American, food guilt may have meant illicitly eating meat on Fridays or failing to achieve membership in the "clean plate club." More recently, there has been almost no aspect of food, from its production in polluted factory farms to its hermetic seal to assuage public concern over contaminants, to its ultimate feared appearance on our hips, that has not inspired guilt. Perhaps it all began in childhood when we were exhorted to "think of all the poor, starving children in . . ." in our attempts to finish all the food on our plates. Lappe (1971; 1977) has suggested that early exposure to notions that people do starve in this world makes it easier to bear actual examples of this painful reality later in life. Such exhortations, however, also might have provided the first experience linking food with guilt.

Eating as an Issue of Trust

At the close of the twentieth century, some of those studying food as metaphor have taken a philosophical right turn in discussions of the spiritual dimensions of food. In this context, eating truly has been viewed as an issue of trust: trust that one deserves to eat; trust also that the next meal will be there, so there is no need to be a glutton. Moral consideration of gluttony has been different from the usual notions of obesity. Morally speaking, one can be gluttonous without being fat since fatness is not a sin in itself. It is unquenchable craving that has transformed eating into a "sin," or gluttony: "Gluttony and girth are two separate matters. The proof of the pudding of gluttony lies not in the size of the body but in the shape of the soul" (Bringle, 1993, p. 62).[9]

Feminists like Orbach, Roth, and Chernin have been suggesting since at least the 1980s that weight stabilizes best when we let go of striving (craving?) and instead get to know our hungers; it also is important to eat what we want and when we want until we reach, but do not go beyond, the point of fullness. For those of a more spiritual than psychological bent, the final outcome of the eternal struggle with food and body image may have more to do with an inability to trust the future, to let go.

Many writers have spoken of food as metaphor at the close of the century. It sometimes seems as though the intense interest in food at this time allows writers to attribute just about any motive or meaning to food. One fashionable interpretation has been to suggest that feminist revisions of dieting at the close of the century have missed the boat when they talked of dieting as something that is antisocial and curable through the application of social controls (sort of like smoking?) rather than viewing this denial of the body as a physical manifestation of the hungry, empty heart. In this analysis, fat has become a symbol not of the personality, but of the soul, the cluttered, neurotic, immature soul (Tisdale, 1993).[10]

In the end, it may be that the *meaning* of the familiar American ambivalence over food these last fifty years has changed as we have aged. For example, bodily control certainly has been more an issue for middle-aged ex-yuppies anxious about physical and sexual vitality than it ever was for young, omnipotent (even if alienated) hippies: "The new food purism—no cholesterol, more fiber and good (as opposed to bad) fats—is a highly individualistic form of politics perfectly suited to the graying of the baby boom generation as well as the mentality of the Reagan years" (Brumberg, 1990, p. 496).

Chapter 6

Disturbed Eating

Food is a metaphor for women's emotional lives. Food is a barometer for women's feelings about themselves and the world. Food can represent the conflicts a woman experiences in her life, becoming a battleground where a woman struggles to establish control over external forces that she perceives to be dictating her life. In a more positive vein, food can symbolize the nurturance and caring a woman feels toward others. Food can be a vehicle for expressing one's sensuous nature.[1] When a woman feels good about herself, she is in control of food and can appreciate the sensual, pleasurable qualities of what she eats. If she prepares the food she eats, she most likely is even more in touch with this process of nurturing herself.

Previous chapters have documented various cultural, social, and economic forces that have eroded the constructive relationship women have had with food in the past. Food traditionally has been the means by which a woman expressed caring and nurturance for others. Women's connection to food, especially its preparation, changed significantly only after the effects of the industrial revolution percolated throughout American society. Women gradually became more alienated from the healing and nurturant properties of food. Anorexia, bulimia, and compulsive eating became more common as women lost touch with the positive elements of food; food now became the enemy for some women. The disintegration of women's traditional food role has created a condition of dis-ease for many women in America today. Absence of the "identity-anchors" food traditionally provided women has increased their vulnerability to cultural pressures that can lead to eating disturbances.

THE STAFF OF LIFE HITS A QUAGMIRE

Chapter three documented the specific ways the industrial revolution created a market for processed foods. The advent of processed foods began an important and permanent change in the ways women relate to food in this culture. The need to encourage women to buy processed food, rather than to prepare their own "from scratch," created an advertising campaign that ultimately devalued the food women prepared with their own hands. This tendency was exacerbated when bottled baby formula was first mass-marketed in the 1890s. Even mother's own breast milk became inferior to doctor-prescribed or store-bought formula. Both of these economically motivated changes in eating customs helped divorce women from an important traditional source of their identity as primary preparers of their families' food.

By the turn of the nineteenth century, the domestic science movement's tendency to devalue ethnic cuisines and to encourage immigrant women to give up their "old world" cooking styles further ruptured women's connections to their traditional role in the countries where they were born. By the 1920s this influencial social movement resulted in home economics being taught in many high schools; the academic extension of the domestic science movement now reinforced the value of Anglo food and middle-class values as early as the intermediate/secondary school years in the lives of girls and young women.

The domestic science movement also encouraged women to adopt written recipes into their cooking repertoire. Exact amounts that were precisely measured replaced "a little of this and a little of that." The implication here was that women's former more intuitive and creative style of cooking could no longer produce a satisfactory result in the kitchen. Again the message to women was that what they produced themselves was not good enough. It took an outside "authority" to successfully feed one's family. This message is likely to have caused a woman to question her abilities in the kitchen, her potential for creative culinary efforts, and even her adequacy as a mother in providing her newborn's first nutrition in life. Anger at such societal devaluation most often was turned inward where it would remain internalized in the form of depression.

Current feminist interpretation of eating disorders as a reaction to patriarchal oppression makes logical sense. Most feminist writers, however, only emphasize the social, economic, and political effects of women's oppression resulting from patriarchal rule. Sexual abuse goes hand-in-glove with eating disorders, since patriarchy historically legitimatized male sexual privilege with economically dependent women and children. Male (white) sexual privilege also has manifested across color lines as clinicians increasingly become aware of eating disorders among women of color.

However, this feminist interpretation must be expanded. Women, especially those experiencing eating disorders, need to understand the ways women's relationship with food has been manipulated by capitalism, the food industry in particular, over the last hundred or so years. The current "epidemic" of eating disorders is not accidental; it has increased in direct proportion to the growth of food processing and the mass marketing of food. In addition, domestic science, the academic version of the food reform movement, helped sever constructive familial and cultural food ties.

THE FOOD CLICHÉS

What follows are commonly believed clichés about women, food, and body image that perpetuate negative self-evaluations: a perfect setup for eating disturbances among American women.

"I'm Not Good Enough"

Poor self-esteem has become more evident as women's relationships with food have deteriorated over the last 150 years; negative responses about self range from merely questioning one's adequacy in the kitchen to self-hatred fueled by a total lack of personal identity. Loss of self-esteem has been fueled by cultural messages that have judged modern women unable to nurture and provide for their families. Social dictates regarding acceptable body size also have triggered feelings of inadequacy, with depression the likely outcome, and often have been expressed in some sort of eating disturbance.

"I Can't Eat Another Bite"

Even in the nineteenth century it was commonly believed that the body could not reliably judge what needed to be eaten for good health. Food reformers were unanimous in their expectation that proper ladies denied all bodily pleasure, for example eating "just a leaf or two of lettuce" (Shapiro, 1986, p. 217). During these early decades of the twentieth century, meat was considered appropriate only for men while starches and sugars, and small portions at that, were thought to constitute proper food for women. In other words, women were expected to nurture everyone but themselves. Home economics amplified the food reformers' message of denial in American schools throughout the twentieth century.

The domestic science fiction that women had no appetite for food became a peculiar sort of reality in the 1950s when dieting seized the public's consciousness. A belief that dieting could finally master any appetite for food quickly spread throughout America in the headlines of the women's magazines so popular after World War II. A corollary, that women really had no right to food, was an even more destructive hidden message in the expectation that women should diet.[2]

At the same time, however, all human beings do need food both for survival and also to satisfy basic psychological needs for nurturance and reassurance. Therefore, the dieting housewife was captured in a dilemma between denial of her desire for food and the need to gratify important psychological needs with food.

Modern fast food and brand names really began to take off in terms of their popularity among Americans in the 1950s. Anthropologists believe both are attractive to Americans because they satisfy a deep need for the familiar in our eating patterns. The current demand for "comfort food" and the high level of bingeing evident in the eating patterns typical in American culture today are just another expression of this strong human need. O'Neill (1996a) has observed that "the American population's largest weight gain has occurred during the New Age of Dietary Enlightenment" (p. 39). The lack of nutritional composition and the yin/yang swings in mood triggered by the consumption of large amounts of processed food (Colbin, 1986) make it difficult to satisfy this deep need via bingeing. Though they appear to comfort the eater, processed foods actually just perpetuate a state of craving.

Psychologists have suggested that a critically important relationship exists between food and sex for women. By the 1950s, psychoanalytic theory had encouraged the American public to see an appetite for food as a repressed appetite for sex. Therefore women, in essence, were not supposed to like either food or sex very much. At the same time, there always has been a role requirement for women to provide both sustenance and sexual pleasure for others.

The concept of denial of desire while being the object of that desire, aptly explains and frames comments so often made by women engaged in what they perceive to be a losing battle with food. Obsession with food—what one wants to eat, cravings for certain foods, discussion of calories and grams of fat in a desired food, a sense of failure experienced when a forbidden food is consumed—all these sorts of thoughts are flavored with desire beyond normal concerns for adequate nutrition and pleasure in one's anticipated next meal.

Underneath these questions lay the woman's real concern: that she insatiably lusts after both food and sexual pleasure. This message suggests that her body is untrustworthy; if she gives into such powerful desires, there might be no end to the satiation of that desire. This refrain sounds disturbingly familiar to the comments made by many women with issues around food; for example, "I can't eat just a few cookies; once I start, I eat the whole box." A woman saying this knows she cannot trust her body.

Women generally are expected to nurture others with little regard for their own needs for nurturance. To some degree, all women with eating disorders are unable to nurture themselves in ways that do not involve food or eating. A compulsive eater, for example, is stereotyped as a nurturer who knows no boundaries. An anorexic woman cannot be nourished. A bulimic woman cannot sustain the nurturing process; her purges renounce the preceding satisfaction of that need. A woman need not be labeled with one of these three major eating disorders, however, to feel trapped in a double-bind: whether to nurture self or others. As one clinical psychologist has summarized the dilemma, "women, sex and food are the royal triumvirate which populate the pages of women's magazines, whether it be diet desserts, sexual exhortations, or more ways to please the one you love" (Liss-Levinson, 1988, p. 128). It is difficult for any woman to be exposed constantly to these multiple, conflicting media messages without developing some degree of ambivalence about the nurturing aspects of food.

Ambivalence about something so basic to survival as food also explains why diet programs based on a twelve-step philosophy generally are impossible to sustain over a long period of time. If food is the enemy and must be severely regulated for the rest of one's lifetime, it is impossible to achieve a state where one can enjoy food without abusing it.

"I Feel Like a Piece of Meat"

It is a well-established fact in the western world that women are defined by their external, physical appearance (body image) whereas men are defined by what they think or do (actions). The evolution of this cultural standard was the first major step in the objectification of women. Regardless of women's advances in education and various career opportunities over the past thirty years, American culture persists in valuing women primarily on the basis of physical appearance while ignoring accomplishments or abilities.

Stewart (1996) has reported impressive data by Averett and Korenman supporting the above generalizations.These researchers found a $12,445 differential in annual salary between obese and underweight women; even women at medically recommended weights made $1,676 a year less than did underweight women. Stewart is quick to acknowledge that likelihood of marriage probably is the variable most influencing these results. The message is clear-cut: women who are financially successfully must have small bodies; education and ability are less important than physical appearance.

Not much has been recorded about women's thoughts and feelings when new role expectations required them to shift from an exclusively maternal role to a more companionate role in marriage at the beginning of the twentieth century. An emphasis on public behavior, reinforced by the new marriage ideal, further reinforced the importance of women's external appearance and behavior at the expense of the internal, or subjective.

Given that women are defined by external appearance, there is a lot of money to be made in marketing successful appearances. This has been the rationale for the dieting industry; it totally ignores the pain an obsession with dieting and exercise can cause women. Beginning in the 1950s, the dieting industry has grown exponentially into a multibillion-dollar industry. Add profits from the exercise or so-called health industry to this figure, and it quickly becomes apparent that huge profits are possible when one views woman's body as a business opportunity.

"You Look Great; Have You Lost Weight?"

Prior to the turn of the century, Lillian Russell, a substantial woman reported to have weighed 200 pounds, was considered to possess the ideal female body. Russell's popularity coincided with the high point of the Victorian era when the average woman had little or no economic or political power. By the turn of the twentieth century, however, elite society already preferred its women rather thin and frail as a symbol of their social distance from the working classes (Brumberg, 1988).

During the early decades of the twentieth century, smaller bodies also became a requirement for middle-class women. After all, domestic science was part of a more general food reform movement that believed a less voluminous body reflected good nutrition, the importance of newly discovered vitamins, and exercise. By 1920 the more slender image of the Gibson Girl gave way to the boyish flapper who symbolized the new freedoms and political power American women had won that year with passage of their right to vote. Removing corsets and raising hemlines exposed more of a woman's actual body; these fashions, therefore, encouraged flappers to have more athletic, often smaller, bodies.

Slimming down also facilitated a new social expectation for housewives: de-emphasis of the maternal role with a new emphasis on the sexual and social aspects of a wife's partnership with her husband. Seid (1989) has used the term "companionate marriage" to describe this new-style wife who was expected to be the athletic, intellectual, and competitive equal of her husband as well as being his social companion. Slimmer women were believed to be more effective as helpmates in their husbands' social advancement or as status symbols of their husband's financial success in the expanded world of business after World War I.

Women did get out of the house to work in the defense industry during World War II. Work in factories, plants, and mills was physical work that resulted in strong bodies that looked good in the trousers and pants popular among women during war years.

In the aftermath of World War II, however, working women were forced to give up their wartime jobs and were encouraged to consider family obligations their primary work. Housecoats reappeared, and dieting replaced physical exercise in determining body shape. It is interesting to note that the dieting industry began at precisely the point in time when severe social restrictions were reinstated for working- and middle-class women. Now women worried about their weight instead of the war effort.

The middle class expanded once again after the second world war. Great abundance and ease of living also characterized the post-war period so that it was possible for many working- and middle-class Americans to live materially more like the rich. Emulating the slimness of the upper class was one way of educating those with less social status in the use of restraint amidst this growing affluence and availability of food. Public opinion polling early in the 1950s found that the more educated the individual, the greater his or her desire to lose weight. A few brave voices begged to differ, observing that eating provided the same satisfaction for some individuals as the more destructive pleasures of alcohol, drugs, or various pathological behaviors; so why create guilt and shame in individuals pursuing this less harmful pleasure? (Seid, 1989). But such thinkers were definitely in a minority and their voices were effectively silenced in the upcoming decades.

A relationship between lack of social power and women's response to that restriction helps explain women's enthusiasm over both domestic science and dieting programs. At the turn of the twentieth century, the only scientific field of study open to women was domestic science; by design, this was the only area of scientific education women were allowed to control. In a similar fashion at mid-century, the only physical space within the home that women were allowed to control was the kitchen (Wajcman, 1991) where they were expected to employ their primary energies feeding their families in an elaborate and time-consuming fashion. Lacking any social power, women were encouraged to use dieting as a way to establish greater control over their bodies: the only physical space they really controlled. Women's perception of their lack of social control triggered both these endeavors while also permanently changing the ways women ate and felt about food and eating.

The 1960s signaled the second wave of feminism just as the 1920s symbolized the freedoms gained when women got the vote. Just as flappers represented the smaller acceptable body for women of their generation, almost fifty years later Twiggy (5'7" tall, weighing 91 lbs.) initiated a yet more dimunitive body ideal for the liberated women of her decade. These images illustrate the historic connection between acceptable body size and access to power. A social requirement for smaller women's bodies has occurred each time feminism has swelled into a social movement for change in America. It is significant that each time women have gained some economic or political power in this century, they also have been expected to make themselves smaller in stature.

Feminists have known for some time that women never have been expected to "take up too much space." But it seems that American culture enforced this requirement even more rigorously when women moved into a "man's world" as they did both in the 1920s and the 1960s. Perhaps bigger women connote too much feminine power in a world where women actually are attaining some *real* economic and political power. Furthermore, if women are kept in a constant turmoil trying to maintain unrealistically small bodies, they will have less individual and collective energy available for furthering a feminist agenda.

In response to the thin body ideal promoted for women in the 1960s, Brown and Jasper (1993) have commented that "the recommended route to perfecting the female body seemed to be getting rid of it altogether" (p. 26). The emphasis on sexual freedom and a youth culture during the hippie era, with its concomitant exposure of the naked body, was offset by a prepubescent body shape. Differences between the sexes were down-played while, at the same time, a very sexualized, yet innocent, image was projected. Perhaps a reduced emphasis on reproductive potential in the bodies of young women of the 1960s was a reaction to the body ideal of their mothers' generation, and reflects the expanded potential for female accomplishment anticipated by the second wave of feminists. It also is likely that the fact that at least some women were making educational and economic gains at this time served as an impetus for the promotion of powerless little girl fashion ushered in by the Twiggy phenomenon. Her clothing style at least created the illusion that women were not taking up too much space.

The myth that one can never be too thin became an obsession during the 1970s at exactly the same time American women were making real advances in education and the work place. By the late 1980s, anorexic models dominated fashion magazines and advertising just when a new third generation of feminists was making its presence felt.

The last decades of the twentieth century have only intensified social pressure to achieve a thin body ideal. A 1996 poll by *People* magazine (Too fat?, 1996) listed the following evidence to support their expressed concern over the thinness ideal's exacerbation of eating disorders: in 1972, 23 percent of American women said they were dissatisfied with their overall appearance but, by 1996, that figure had more than doubled to approximately one-half of all women expressing frequent dissatisfaction with their bodies; women were three times as likely as men to have negative thoughts about their bodies, with younger women most likely to manifest this tendency; since 1979, Miss America contestants have become so skinny that the majority now are at least 15 percent below the recommended body weight for their height; nationally the reported incidence of both anorexia and bulimia has doubled since 1970, according to data from the American Psychiatric Association.

The late twentieth century demand that women maintain small, hard bodies has encouraged devotion to exercise regimes, individual diets, organized weight-reduction programs, and even adaptation of twelve-step programs, such as Overeaters Anonymous, to control "food addiction." Obsession with unrealistically small bodies has become a perfect breeding ground for the development of eating disorders. A cult of thinness has affected women's basic health and reproductive capacities; 20 percent of women who exercise regularly to maintain a thin, muscular body reportedly are amenorrheal (Seid, 1989).

A 1996 study at the University of Arizona found that the more time undergraduate women spent watching television and reading health, fitness, beauty, and fashion magazines, the more likely they were to idealize thinness, dislike their own bodies, and show symptoms of eating disorders (McLaughlin, 1996). These researchers have suggested that implementing feminist principles might discourage the development of eating disturbances.

Though some who have written about women's body image generally applaud women's entrance into the gym and organized athletics, others are concerned that some women have used this sort of purging as a means of maintaining normal weight while binge eating large amounts of food. Such a practice could be considered a new category of eating disorder that could be labeled "exercise bulimia."[3]

It is important to encourage young women to value their accomplishments and see themselves as competent individuals capable of managing their own lives, women who accept and nurture their physical bodies, whatever shape or size they might be. All these qualities are inversely related to the development of disturbed eating patterns.

"Only White Girls Have Eating Disorders"

The pressure to be thin works harder on women in some ethnic and racial categories than others. It is important to factor socioeconomic status and exposure to western white culture into any prediction of body image conflict for women of color around the world.

Anorexia and bulimia have long been thought to occur much more often among the so-called privileged white women who live in western industrialized countries; consequently, these eating disorders have often been overlooked or misdiagnosed among black and hispanic American women by trained researchers (Silber, 1986). There is almost no research literature available on the incidence of eating disorders among Asian American women.

Because of ignorance and self-fulfilling prophecies in the research literature, it is not suprising that what appear to be contradictory trends have been observed among black American women. Chambers (1995), for example, has suggested younger black women are experiencing increased pressure to achieve the slim straight lines of today's dominant fashionable body image.[4] The existence of greater fat-oppressive attitudes among young middle-class black women at the turn of the twenty-first century most likely is a racial variant of what Brown and Jasper (1993) have identified as an indicator of assimilation and acculturation. Their description of an immigrant woman who valued fat in her children as a symbol of being well fed and healthy often is the grandmother of the bulimic woman who hates and fears her genetically generated "zoftig" breasts and thighs.

Much of the literature on body image along with messages from popular black culture, on the other hand, suggest a greater acceptance of full-figured women in black American culture.[5] A 1995 University of Arizona survey of black high school students found that 70 percent of teenage African-American girls were satisfied with their bodies (Too fat?, 1996).

Perhaps the popular notion that women of color have greater license to maintain larger bodies explains why many well-trained professionals have misdiagnosed eating disorders among black and hispanic women; such errors in diagnosis may have resulted because of researchers' assumption that eating disorders are the province of middle- and upper-class white women (Silber, 1986).

It has been reported that the "ideal" woman in many African and some Asian cultures still is buxom and curvaceous (Shroff, 1993). Such an ample body standard may explain why the incidence of anorexia and bulimia so far have been much more prevalent in western industrialized countries: "Where food is scarce, a larger woman is sought after. When food is plentiful, a thinner woman seems to be sought after" (p. 110).

"I'd Rather Be Dead Than Fat"

It is a well-established fact that anorexia nervosa has been institutionalized as acceptable behavior for women for centuries, if not millenia. In her historical study of anorexia, Brumberg (1988) reported that institutionalized anorexic behavior in western culture has existed in Europe since at least the middle ages. Bulimia was first described as a means of weight control in the American popular press in 1936, but, like anorexia, it has been institutionalized in some form since at least the time of the Romans' debaucherous dinners. Even though anorexia nervosa was introduced as a diagnostic category in western medicine during the latter part of the nineteenth century, the so-called epidemic of eating disorders usually is thought to have emerged in America during the 1970s. Throughout the last decades of the twentieth century, anorexia, bulimia, compulsive eating and what might be called exercise bulimia increasingly have been identified as efficient methods for maintaining the small body idealized in modern society.

The American Anorexia/Bulimia Association estimates that 6 percent of American women now have one or both of these eating disorders; 1996 statistics indicate that 30 to 50 percent of anorexic women will go in and out of hospitals and treatment centers; 10 to 20 percent of the women who are hospitalized will die (Ross, 1996).

Some feminists (Chernin, 1981, 1985; Orbach, 1978; Thompson, 1992, 1994) have analyzed eating disorders as a reaction to the "culture of thinness" model that today pervades affluent, privileged countries. As we have seen, the standard of thinness has become greater with each decade or two in the twentieth century. Seid (1989) has suggested that anorexia is simply the extreme form of a continuum of food deprivation behaviors occurring in ever-increasing numbers of American women. Brown and Jasper (1993) have associated the increased incidence of anorexia with women's greater participation in the labor force as a result of the second wave of feminism.

Thompson (1992) has suggested that explanations for eating disorders that focus primarily on cultural demands for thinness imply that it is the woman's "obsession" with appearance that best explains the problem. How then can we explain the appearance of eating disorders in women raised in families or ethnic communities that value larger women? Such an interpretation not only creates more shame and guilt for the middle- and upper-class women constructed as self-centered and vain, but it also portrays working-class white women and women of color as detached and unaffected by dominant standards of beauty. Another implication is that these allegedly unaffected women are just one step away from being hungry and, therefore, not susceptible to eating problems when, in reality, they may binge as a means of coping with poverty. Consideration of the intersections of race, class, sexuality, and gender exposes the demeaning attributes of femininity as it currently is constructed in middle-class terms. The existence of anorexia and bulimia across all these categories suggests that these illnesses actually are serious responses to social injustices.

Most feminists studying eating disturbances have concluded that the overwhelming oppression of patriarchy best explains the majority of eating disorders seen among all sorts of women both in America and other cultures around the world. Chernik (1995) has described dramatically the impact a feminist analysis of eating disorders had on her own recovery from anorexia:

> As long as society resists female power, fashion will call healthy women physically flawed. As long as society accepts the physical, sexual and economic abuse of women, popular culture will prefer women who resemble little girls. Sitting in the hospital the summer after my college graduation, I grasped the absurdity of a nation of adult women dying to grow small. . . . Gaining weight and getting my head out of the toilet bowl was the most political act I have ever committed. (p. 81)

One aspect of patriarchal oppression is sexual abuse of young girls and women. Several feminist therapists have written of the strong correlation between sexual abuse earlier in life and subsequent eating disorders.[6] Body numbness and a more extreme disassociation from one's body that often occurs in reaction to sexual abuse is mimicked in the "out of body" sensation that often accompanies bingeing, purging, and the starvation of anorexia.

Women experiencing eating disorders often emphasize control as a satisfying accompaniment of extreme exercise regimes, purging, or starving their bodies. These activities create the illusion of being in control of oneself even though these women may perceive little personal control in other areas of their lives.

"Fatty, Fatty, Two-by-Four"

Fat oppression comes in many forms. Generally it involves messages from society that pressure an individual to be thinner or, if that is impossible, erode the self-esteem of women who are larger in size. The Lillian Russells of the world have been challenged by women embodying the new slim, athletic ideal.

Levenstein's (1988) historical analysis of society at the turn of the last century documented the oppressive messages about body fat that Americans first were exposed to at that time. Slimmer bodies began to be appreciated in the first two decades of the twentieth century. Concerns about physical fitness also emerged at this time. The Gibson Girl was born and, after the first world war, a nymph-like ideal emerged, one bordering on preadolescent boyishness.

Shapiro (1986) has shown us how dieting and caloric intake became the focus of discussions in middle-class homes at this time, replacing discussions of books, social events, and families. Fat oppression infiltrated women's lives during the next several decades of the century. Concern over weight, when combined with the social pressure on women to run the household with a minimal outlay of servants, resulted in housewives minimizing meals, which, in turn, led to a trend toward lighter, simpler foods.

There was a growing obsession with slimness as the decades passed. Women now certainly could not be "too rich or too thin." Fat was the enemy; then food was the enemy; deprivation was the cure. Excess weight conjured up images of heart disease, diabetes, and obesity, whereas slimness was associated with good health and attractiveness. These perceptions now carried the weight of supposedly scientific research.

The term *fat oppression* was first used in a special issue of a feminist therapy journal devoted to the topic (Brown and Rothblum, 1989). Fat oppression denoted society's systematic offensive against larger women or, for that matter, any woman who could be made to feel she was too large. One of the journal's editors, in fact, suggested that even feminist therapists, generally sensitive to various forms of discrimination, often were guilty of the same internalized fat-phobic beliefs that dominated the general population in their treatment of larger women (Brown and Rothblum, 1989). Feminist therapists were reminded that most fat people are healthy and at less risk from their larger size than they were from dieting and the negative and prejudicial attitudes of others. The situation when a client in feminist therapy experienced an increase in self-esteem as a result of weight reduction reminded the editors of the chillingly analogous pre-feminist literature in which women learned to "accept their femininity" and become happier as a result. In other words, a client's rise in self-esteem in such a circumstance might be more a measure of that client's acceptance of a destructive societal norm regarding acceptable body size than an indication of the client's comfort with her basic self, regardless of body size. This observation served as a reminder that the literature on weight and body size increasingly has supported an anti–fat-oppressive perspective, and that fat people often are as fit and healthy as non-fat people. Even though the true health risks regarding weight lie at only the extreme low and high ends of the weight continuum, our culture has focused only on the health risks at the upper end of the weight continuum.

In several books on eating and body size in contemporary America, Chernin (1981, 1985) has viewed fat oppression as a conspiracy to keep women from developing their bodies, appetites, and personal/collective power. If women grow too large, they will be seen as too powerful; so society minimizes women's images, reduces the fat in food, and tells women that they must slim down. An analogy might exist between women in America, who are socialized to be small in stature and devoid of personal power, and women in traditional China whose bound feet crippled them in the name of beauty. American women have, in effect, been crippled by fat oppression. Chernin believes that fat oppression has contributed to a contradiction in our society whereby women are told they must strive for personal power while continuing to be small in size. Women simultaneously are told to expand their horizons, broaden their minds, enlarge their views, assert themselves, and gain self-esteem *plus* lose weight, diet, reduce fat, lose inches, restrict food intake, and drop a couple of dress sizes. Social dictates, therefore, suggest that every woman who loses weight will overcome misogyny, that her social problems will become lighter, and that the business world will welcome her. Chernin says women are not encouraged to change the culture so that they might be accepted into it *as is*. Rather women are encouraged to spend their lives anguishing over their failure to lose weight and modify their bodies in accordance with cultural norms. After all, culture rewards those who comply with its standards. One way of handling this simultaneous, contradictory message has been to make the problematic message part of something outside the individual.[7]

The contradictory message of fat oppression and the human need to indulge is quite apparent in the food pages of our major national newspapers and women's magazines.[8] Fat oppression also can be seen in food labeling and advertisements that accompany, and finance, the weekly food section of the newspaper. Women certainly are under pressure to be thinner and yet, at the same time, are being told by articles in this section that every now and then it is alright to indulge. This message, however, contradicts everything society has taught women about minimizing, depriving, and slimming down. Fat oppression then is just another way to keep women fighting upstream against a roller coaster of societal expectations which, in turn, keep women themselves in an oppressed state.

The bias against fat is especially virulent in attitudes toward fat children who are often referred to as "ugly" and "stupid." One study (*Sojourner*, 1994) found that adults would prefer a child with an obvious disability, such as blindness or crippling, rather than a child who simply was fat. A 1995 study in Boston found that, when obese people were asked which they'd prefer, going blind or regaining weight, nearly 90 percent said they would rather be blind (Foreman, 1995).

The advent of "fat camps" for children reflects the intolerance parents and the general society have felt for children considered overweight. A seven-week summer camp costing several thousand dollars is dramatic evidence of the degree of fat phobia some parents sustain in contemporary culture (Perrin, 1991). The editor of a major university's diet and nutrition newsletter has explained that a weight-reduction regimen, no matter how it's constructed, involves giving a person less food than she or he would voluntarily eat. Because children want to please their parents, they end up feeling there is something wrong with them for wanting to eat more than their parents want to give. Rather than shipping the child off to a camp designed to make weight loss the child's summer accomplishment, it has been suggested that parents work on nutrition within the household by creating a positive role model in terms of their own behavior. Fat camps reinforce fat phobia while lowering a child's sense of self-worth (Lindner, 1991).

When the degree of fat phobia and the rejection of fat individuals in our culture is considered, it makes logical sense that the majority of women in our culture have invested considerable energy in maintaining a thin body. Eating disorders are a natural extension of this obsession with thinness. Fat oppression is just one expression of the more pervasive oppression any woman experiences in our culture.[9]

WOMEN AND APPETITE: A FEMINIST ANALYSIS

Fat oppression is a powerful theme in America. There are all sorts of subtle and not-so-subtle messages being thrown at women everyday.[10] Equal opportunities exist as long as women have the body size that society dictates is beautiful and powerful, also one that is nearly impossible to maintain. Even though women are gaining some power in society, they are expected to take up even less physical space. Staying thin means looking younger which has been women's primary value under patriarchy since youth equals reproductive vulnerability. Women are considered shameful when they get big because their size is now a sign of failure, whereas larger men signify greater personal power. Metaphorically food and eating behavior may reflect how well or poorly a woman is relating emotionally with others. The cultural press for thinness only increases the likelihood of conflicting messages that encourage eating disorders.

Feminist interpretations of eating disturbances are more empowering than earlier attempts to explain eating disorders as evidence of an individual's pathology. Clinicians' tendency to view anorexia, bulimia, and compulsive eating as separate categories of illness stresses differences among these eating issues and implies a distinct pathology for each category of eating disorder. Viewing each type of eating disorder as a point along a continuum, shared also by women who have disturbed eating but have not been diagnosed with an eating disorder, emphasizes the commonalities among all these disturbed eating situations. The fact that many women with one eating disorder will shift to another over time or exhibit more than one eating disorder at the same time lends credence to the continuum view of eating disorders.

But explaining eating disturbances primarily as the fault of our cultural obsession with thinness ignores the wider context of patriarchal oppression that also promotes eating disorders in other ways. Sexual abuse, for instance, is a major factor in the etiology of eating disorders while also providing a cornerstone of patriarchal oppression. Even women who otherwise have benefited from improved gender equality in our society do not feel they can guarantee their personal safety in this allegedly gentler, kinder society. In addition to all the women diagnosed with eating disorders, many, many other women in our culture exercise rigid control over their food intake to maintain acceptably small bodies, believing that they can maintain control of at least one area of their lives.

Chapter 7

Healing Ourselves with Food

In addition to losing control over the nutritional components of the food we eat, the very act of *losing control* is psychologically uncomfortable for most women with eating issues. As discussed in the previous chapter, past sexual abuse, a common denominator for many women with eating disorders, connotes a similar loss of control. Keeping the importance of personal control in mind, it does not make sense to further give up control of one's body in terms of the food eaten, to nourish and maintain the body.

The previous chapter also discussed the various ways body image is linked to eating disorders. It is well established in the literature that body image pressures have contributed greatly to the development of eating issues in American women, especially younger ones. Though the relationship between media messages encouraging abnormally thin bodies and eating disorders has been demonstrated in at least one research study (McLaughlin, 1996), only late in the twentieth century have there been signs that the American public is willing to question such an abnormal, potentially destructive standard for young women.

One tenet of feminism is that the personal truly is political. This belief has been quite useful in designing successful therapeutic treatments for modern women. It is only natural, therefore, to look to the ways we can heal ourselves and our damaged and sometimes pathological relationships with food. After all, women originally were the healers, using foodstuffs and other herbs and "natural" remedies in these efforts. This chapter explores the psychological framework feminist therapy utilizes in the treatment of eating disorders today; also considered are some recent and ancient ways individuals have accomplished this healing.

IN SUPPORT OF REAL BODIES

An encouraging early sign of grass-roots refusal to accept "anorexic marketing" was the 1996 decision by a support group for mothers of anorexic daughters to boycott products sold through anorectic advertising.[1]

That same year, an exclusive watchmaker withdrew advertising from *Vogue* magazine because the watch company believed models in this publication were of "anorexic proportions" (McPhee, 1996). This decision set a precedent since, for the first time, an advertiser, rather than consumers, made a decision with economic consequences for a business dependent on advertising income. Omega's decision created possibilities for other constructive corporate responses to the endless "buck passing" fashion and entertainment industries engage in when discussing their role in the development of eating disorders.[2]

Media's Mixed Messages

In the late 1990s, the *New York Times* began using "real" women with varied careers, ages, racial/ethnic backgrounds, and sizes for their semi-annual "Fashions of the Times" editions.[3] How much the rationalization for their new choice of models was related to that year's incipient protest by advertisers over the use of "anorexic" models in fashion magazines is impossible to ascertain. But therapists and others concerned with distorted presentations of female bodies were encouraged by the sensitive, thoughtful editorial behavior of this major "voice" in the world of fashion.

Another hopeful indicator involved the publication by a weekly news magazine of a major report on America's mixed advertising, fashion, and entertainment industry messages about body size. After sampling the literature on body image and health professionals' responses to this conflicting message, *People* magazine revealed the results of their 1996 poll, commissioned expressly for their cover story (Too fat?, 1996). Not suprisingly, they found that one-half of all women reported frequent dissatisfaction with their appearance. It is interesting to note that, even though distress over one's body image is an overwhemingly feminine condition, *People*'s feature story focused much of their text on male concerns with body image. Was this an attempt to give equal time to men's concerns, or was it a ploy to seem inclusive in their reporting? The coverage concluded with the reassuring observation that people actually yearn to be around people who are comfortable "in their own skin." Hopefully, this statement conveyed the message that it is not self-alienating for individuals to opt out of the mass effort to attain the unrealistic body image the mass media constantly thrusts upon the American public.

It is critically important to continue publicizing this message to women and girls: the body image generally presented in the advertising, fashion, and entertainment industries is unrealistic and, therefore, not appropriately viewed as a model for any individual woman's personal appearance goals. As even those in the entertainment industry argue, the bodies seen on the screen and in magazines represent an "ideal," and are not intended to convey any expectation for real women's actual body proportions. In the late twentieth century, the average height and weight of an American woman was 5'4" and 142 pounds, while the average height and weight of a model was 5'9"and 110 pounds (Too fat?, 1996). It clearly is unrealistic, therefore, to expect any woman to possess the same body proportions as are modeled in fashion magazines.

What such discussion of ideal versus actual body proportions has ignored, however, is the fact that models and movie stars *are* the role models for many younger American women. These stars set the standard by which many women measure themselves. The *People* cover story set a constructive precedent in this magazine's effort to reach the average American woman or girl who has been caught up in an unrealistic struggle to look like her role models in magazines, movies, and television. Since teenagers and young adult women are more likely to read a weekly news magazine than an academic text, the *People* coverage was a perfect vehicle for reaching the target group.

Diets Don't Do It

Sooner or later most women turn to diets as one means of adapting their bodies to look more like the role models in the print and visual media whom they emulate. A cursory examination of the tabloids in any supermarket suggests that diets are the most commonly chosen means for reducing body size. It is unlikely that a woman thinks first of *permanent* ways to modify her diet as a means of modifying body size: "There is this thing that healthy eating is punishment, that it can't taste good and be good for you" (Kagan, 1990, p. 8). Women with this attitude are unlikely to think that so-called healthy eating can be a long-term, enjoyable experience leading to a more desirable body size.

It would be helpful for women to realize how much income their unrealistic body image expectations have generated for the dieting industry in America. In 1970, diet industry revenues were $10 billion whereas, by 1996, their revenues had jumped to $33 billion (Too fat?, 1996). The diet industry has made huge sums of money from women's exaggerated concern over their physical appearance. In some cases the same corporation sells both the food that fattens women up and the dieting program for them to lose the same weight. The H. J. Heinz Company, for example, has owned Weight Watchers since 1978. No one likes to feel manipulated and perhaps even "cheated" out of her own good money. Getting across this message might help women become angry enough to make the "personal political" and collectively refuse to continue being exploited for the sake of a profit margin. Eighty percent of all American women diet on a regular basis (Too fat?, 1996). If this group chose instead to modify their eating behavior permanently in less radical ways to achieve a desirable body image, a considerable amount of personal income would be saved and made available for more constructive personal expenditures.

RECONNECTING WITH FOOD

The previous chapter suggested cultural reasons why women are likely to deny their food desires. A critically important task for women working to resolve eating issues is to accept their *right* to nourish themselves with food. Acceptance at a deeper level does not occur, however, just because a woman has been exposed intellectually to the notion that she has a right to savor and enjoy the food she consumes. This right usually must be experienced over and over again in her actual consumption of food.

How Full Is Full?

Several self-help books on eating issues in the popular press make this point (Chernin, 1981, 1985; Orbach, 1978; Roth, 1982, 1984, 1991) and have provided specific exercises and self-reports to engage the reader in the *experience* of allowing herself to enjoy the food actually consumed. Roth has gone so far as to suggest that her readers eat anything they want, *but only to the point of feeling satisfied or full without satiation.*

Knowing when one is full can be an important learning experience for a woman with eating issues. It is not a common phenomenon in American culture to experience hunger; usually American bellies have food in them. Many adults in American culture were raised to "eat everything on your plate." Such instruction teaches children to override internal hunger and fullness cues; this instruction also results in adults who have lost touch with their "natural self-regulation of calorie intake and may encourage a lifelong propensity to overeat" (Drexler, 1996). "All-you-can-eat" is a peculiarly American phrase and, since the nation's founding, citizens have worked hard to keep hunger at bay.[4]

Most Americans eat more on the basis of habit or time of day than because their stomachs communicate a need for nourishment. Because of the ready availability of food and a tendency for Americans at the turn of the twenty-first century to eat alone, food can be used to satisfy many psychological needs totally unrelated to the nourishment aspect of eating. We eat when we are anxious, angry, lonely, bored: all legitimate psychological states that deserve attention and action. But eating as a response to any of these feelings is inappropriate and an abuse of the biologically intended purpose of eating.

So accomplishing Roth's dictum to eat only to the point of feeling full may not be as easy as it first appears, especially when practiced by a woman with eating issues. But developing an awareness of the body's *needs* is an important first step in determining the best ways to satisfy those needs in a rational manner that also maintains harmony between mind and body. If a woman has repeated experiences of acknowledging "legitimate" need and satisfying that need through her own efforts to feed herself, she then observes that such behavior does not have negative consequences in terms of body image or destructive eating behaviors. This chain of events will help her realize a growing confidence in her own ability to care for herself without adverse consequences.

When Food Is the Enemy

There is a growing tendency on the part of all Americans to view food in an adversarial manner. The editor of a major American culinary publication, for example, has observed that people feel so confused, guilty, and afraid at the table, that what used to be a source of great joy, fun, pleasure, and emotional sustenance, now is a place of great discomfort (Kagan, 1990). This sort of attitude has created a negative backdrop for efforts to reconnect with food in a positive manner.

Fortunately, there is a coalition building between the taste and health communities to promote exciting, sophisticated food in conjunction with healthy eating. A new magazine entitled *Eating Well* debuted in 1990 and was an immediate commercial success. The editor has stated that one of the tenets of the magazine has been the belief that food that is good for you need not offend the taste buds. The magazine was founded in response to many diets that are healthy, "but no one in their right minds could live on" (Kagan, 1990, p. 10).

TAKING CONTROL

Any endorsement for satisfying one's nutritional needs by personally taking charge of provisions in a healthy, positive manner must be juxtaposed with the the *fact* that it increasingly is unlikely that any Americans will prepare their own food.

Doesn't Anyone Know How to Cook Anymore?

As early as 1988, statistics revealed that only 15 percent (a reduction of 35 percent from fifteen years earlier) of all Americans still basically prepared all their own food, often from whole ingredients (Belasco, 1989). By 1996 Americans were spending more than half their food budget on food they did not prepare themselves (Drexler, 1996).

Eating food prepared by others involves someone else making decisions on ingredients, flavor, and texture, and allows the individual consuming the food to be truly ignorant of what she is eating. Fewer types of food make up the total caloric intake of younger Americans in comparison with older folks' array of foods eaten. Regardless of the variety of foods eaten, however, Americans as a whole do not eat a nutritionally balanced diet (Drexler, 1996). Perhaps the very abundance of cheap food at the end of the twentieth century has caused food to lose much of its value for Americans.

In addition to losing control of the nutritional properties of the food we eat, the very act of *losing control* is psychologically uncomfortable for many women with eating issues. As discussed in the previous chapter, past sexual abuse, a common denominator for many women with eating disorders, connotes a similar loss of control. Keeping the importance of personal control in mind, it logically does not make sense for the individual to give up further control of her body, in terms of the food eaten to nourish and maintain that body, by reliance on others to provide one's food.

Clearly there is a trend to eat alone or "on the run" for most American families. What is lost with the increased tendency for eating to be a "solo ritual" is the social control and support that meals traditionally provided.[5]

The early 1990s saw the beginning of a trend for fast food restaurants to take over the food delivery systems of American public schools and the cafeterias of our institutions of higher learning (Cobb, 1994). Critics have argued that having McDonald's, for example, provide school lunches is nothing more than public education providing a training ground for future consumers of Big Macs and other such products. Supporters have argued that this is the food kids want and will eat, therefore, why not provide food that, at least, actually will be eaten by students at lunchtime.

In response, the federal government has conducted a pilot program whereby middle-school students studied nutrition and then participated in the creation of menus for their school lunch program. This successful program has spawned similar programs at public schools around the country (Daley, 1994; Julian, 1997; Reichl, 1995). Because students have an educated input into the decisions determining the actual food they eat at school, such programs are a stellar example of one way to teach children early and realistically the skills they need to make healthy food choices for themselves throughout their lives. Because they are making the decisions themselves, it also is much more likely these students actually will eat the healthy food on their plates at lunchtime.

Food as the Connection

Mintz has commented perceptively that solo eating for adults provides a real analogy to sensuality: "We assume that adults think the act of love involves other people—and many societies think the act of eating involves other people" (Drexler, p. 24). Mintz' observation reinforces the previous chapter's assertion that eating disorders really are a disorder of desire: a disruption in the ability to satisfy one's sexual and eating desires that afflicts many contemporary American women.

It is interesting to note that women with eating issues almost always cast their problems with food in an isolated context. The battle exists between food and them alone; there are no other principal players in that battle in their mind's eye. Reinstating eating as a social event, perhaps even a celebration of the food being eaten, helps to recast eating as an activity to be shared with others, no longer a lone battle between woman and the enemy (read: food).

Preparing food for others as a way of expressing love and caring has traditionally been part of women's role in western culture. Previous chapters documented modifications in women's role that resulted in a break in this positive connection with food for women. Perhaps one way to regain the comfort and positive self-regard that traditional food roles gave is for women to take a more active hand in the preparation of the food they both eat themselves and offer to those they love. This strategy not only would satisfy psychological needs for nurturing self and others, but taking control of food preparation also would allow women to make nutritional decisions about the food they actually consume on a meal-by-meal basis.

Even written recipes, first introduced by the domestic science movement in America as useful guides for successful cooking, have become a tyranny in women's attempts to feed their families in a healthy and tasteful manner. Written recipes definitely can make a cook unsure of her own instincts and can cause her to experience a loss of confidence in her perception of herself as adequate in the kitchen: "A slavish devotion to recipes robs people of the kind of experiential knowledge that seeps into the brain meal after meal, day after day, over a lifetime of cooking" (O'Neill, 1996b). In addition, the energy it takes to scrupulously adhere to a recipe is at odds with the creative flow needed to execute a dish with heart and soul. In other words a woman might have to abandon the rules of cooking and, armed with some basic knowledge of nutrition, forge her own unique path to enjoyable, healthy cooking for herself and others who matter in her life.

Actual food preparation provides a positive way to reconnect with one's ability to nourish and nurture oneself and loved ones with food. Because this role has been seen as a duty or "drudgery" for women in the twentieth century, it is imperative to reconstruct women's relationship with food now at the approach of the twenty-first century.

It was previously mentioned how Julia Child spearheaded a renewed love affair with French cuisine in America during the 1960s; it is interesting that Julia Child has been publicized as "the feminist we'll remember" in the latter 1990s (Lydon, 1996).[6] Child's importance as a positive role model for women nurturing themselves and others with food apparently was the basis for this conclusion: "What Julia Child did [was] deconstruct this French, classical, rule-based cooking tradition and make it accessible to women as a source of pleasure at home" (p. 11). In addition to her association with good eating, Child also has been identified as a spokesperson for moderation in nutrition; witness her refrain: the food one prepares should contain "a little bit of everything because you never know what you might be missing that was important to your nutrition . . . and have a good time . . . this is French wisdom" (p. 14). It is important to keep positive role models, such as Child, prominent in the American press as a counterpoint to the much more publicized message these days of denial and suspicion, of food as enemy.

ALTERNATIVE EATING

The ambivalence Americans express toward healthy food is apparent in any analysis of food behavior changes over the last twenty-five years. Americans overall have made some positive dietary changes in response to nutritional updates from the federal government and other public information regarding nutrition.

What Americans Are Eating

Over the last quarter-century, our annual consumption of fresh fruit has jumped from 77 pounds per person to 97 pounds per person. Fresh vegetable consumption has gone from 79 pounds to 105 pounds. Butter and egg intake have dropped. Red meat consumption plummeted initially, but began increasing again in the 1990s. Poultry consumption has dropped even though many Americans are substituting chicken for beef in their diet. At the same time, however, the milk we drink continues to be the less healthful 2-percent milkfat or whole milk. Cheese consumption has doubled, and we are loading up on more sugar and other refined sweeteners than ever. We drink five times more soda than fruit juice. We are eating more grains, but tend to consume them in snacks rather than whole food dishes such as pasta (Drexler, 1996).

In a 1996 survey by the Food Marketing Institute, shoppers in the American capital were asked what aspects of the food they ate most concerned them nutritionally. Sixty percent said lower fat content was their main goal. Only three percent cited getting a balanced diet even though most nutrition experts say a balanced diet is the key to good nutrition.

Current nutritional guidelines for a balanced diet as determined by the FDA have been highly publicized by the government using a food "pyramid" to visually represent the foods that should be eaten each day. The number of servings per food group are intended to facilitate the correct food choices required for a balanced diet each day. The fact that the protein level of the current pyramid still is only represented by meat, egg, and dairy choices in 1996 (with the exception of the small bowl of kidney beans in the "meat" group in some pyramid representations), is indicative of the continuing influence the meat and dairy industries have on FDA policy.[7]

Beyond USDA Guidelines

Colbin (1986) has developed an alternative theory of nutrition based on traditional Asian medicine that emphasizes the "expansive" and "contractive" properties of the foods we eat. In order to minimize food cravings, it is desirable to try and maintain a relative balance between eating at the two extremes of the food continuum. Expansive foods are those that tend to release physical energy and body heat. They are foods derived from the above-ground growing parts of plants: fruits and other simple sugars; nuts and other fats; grains; leaves; shoots; and alcohol. Contractive foods derive from the base and roots of plants: potatoes; carrots; salts; and sea vegetables. Most complex carbohydrates are centrally positioned in Colbin's explanation of this alternative evaluation of food properties. Eating only expansive *or* contractive foods may cause an imbalance within the body. The standard American diet of processed, fast food, however, is very heavily expansive: "We eat junk food, and ... tend to eat and eat and eat that and not be satisfied," the head of a major cooking school in New York City has observed, concerning the need to find a balance between nutrition and taste in the food we eat (Kagan, 1990, p. 12).

What Colbin and other members of the food industry concerned with balance in one's diet are reacting to is the tendency for the diet of contemporary Americans to encourage food cravings or a state of imbalance or so-called disharmony.

The goal of nutrition and other healing treatments in Asian medicine is to correct a "pattern of disharmony" (Kaptchuk, 1982) that has created imbalance within the human organism. Applying these principles to eating disorders, the disturbed individual could be described as having an imbalance in yang (expansive) and yin (contractive) tendencies in the body and mind. It is important to emphasize the requirement that the *whole* organism be considered in this system of treatment. Treatment of women with eating issues, therefore, would not just focus on their diet, behavior, *or* psychological state; rather all three would be dealt with in any treatment incorporating the principles of authentic Asian medicine.

Women with eating issues often are eating heavily on the "expansive" end of the food continuum, since these foods are often perceived as being "lite" and low in calories in western systems of dieting. Expansive eating, however, tends to create volatile emotions, a feeling of being "out of control," and eating binges. Most diets emphasize expansive foods such as greens, fruit, raw vegetables, and pasta and other grains or rice. In warmer climes this diet might suffice, giving proper nutrition without encouraging a feeling of being "out of control." But such a diet, especially in the northern parts of America during the colder months of the year, will cause an excessively expansive condition that is likely to create psychologically "out-of-control" feelings.

Chapter 8

Transposing the Personal and Political

Enloe (1989) has suggested that energy moves in at least two directions: social forces influence individuals, but personal initiative also can shape social policy. American women can transform distorted relationships with food into healthy affirmations of feminine initiative; this is an expression of the "personal" reflecting the "political." At the same time, individuals can register their political preferences while engaging in the mundane act of eating; this is an expression of "political" reality being restructured by "personal" choice.

THE PERSONAL AS POLITICAL: APPETITE FOR CHANGE

In my experience, the successful treatment of eating issues is possible when the principles for healing discussed in the previous chapter are incorporated into a group therapy framework.[1] Effective treatment, therefore, must help women to change both their thinking and behavior regarding food. The following discussion of this unique therapy group illustrates one successful application of the personal as political.

Appetite for Change is the name the therapist selected for the four-hour weekly evening meeting of a small group of women experiencing disturbed relationships with food. Most of the group members considered themselves to have an "eating disorder," and all of the women actively sought professional treatment for their "illnesses" prior to joining Appetite for Change. Each evening's meeting provided three distinct experiences for the women: a therapeutic experience in the initial ninety-minute group process session, an educational experience in the therapist's subsequent presentation of nutritional material relevant to the evening's meal plus hands-on culinary instruction in the preparation of the meal; and a dining experience when the entire group finally sat down to enjoy the meal they had jointly prepared.

Transforming Distorted Relationships with Food

Talking about one's issues with food may act as a palliative; talking is not very effective, however, in the modification of actual eating behavior. An environment that encourages experimentation with diet, nutritional information, and culinary competency does correlate with changes in eating behavior. A woman must be given an opportunity, therefore, to prepare the food she would like to be eating. She also must have the opportunity to sit down and eat this food in a nurturing, supportive environment.

Because therapy traditionally groups women on the basis of clinical diagnosis, treatment often prevents a woman with a particular eating disorder from seeing the connection between her disorder and those of women with different clinical diagnoses. Individual therapy also does not provide opportunities for women to nurture one another in the process of healing themselves. Appetite for Change was designed to avoid these pitfalls of traditional therapy and to encourage integration, both within and with other women, in several different ways.

Women with different eating disorder labels are grouped together in Appetite for Change. Mixing together women with different eating issues allows members to realize the commonalities they all share. This important learning is useful in the group's eventual analysis of causal factors underlying disturbed relationships with food (as analyzed in preceding chapters). Empathic support of other women is facilitated while the "divide and conquer" mentality commonly reflected in contemporary discussion of eating disorders is discouraged.

Women with eating disorders traditionally have had specific, unrelated treatment options: participation in individual or group therapy, cooking classes, or a course in nutrition. Appetite for Change integrates all these activities into one therapeutic process.

Women can enter or leave the group as dictated by their individual needs; in this way the group reflects women's relationships in real life where individuals continually enter and leave our lives. Commitment to the group is ensured, however, since each member contracts in advance to join the group for a set period of time; each segment of Appetite for Change lasts a few months. This policy protects the integrity of the group as a whole.

Women with eating issues regularly refer to their bodies as separate entities from their minds. Self-description of this sort reflects a detrimental mind/body split in the psyche. The varied experiences of Appetite for Change encourage women to reunite mind and body, both in their thinking and behavior pertaining to food.

Appetite for Change encourages change in women's relationships with food in several different ways. The therapist actively educates group members about the historical antecedents for eating disorders in American culture (see Chapters 3, 4, and 5). Emphasis also is given to the ways American culture has promoted a dissolution of positive food associations that, at least some women, experienced as young children. Group analysis from a feminist perspective evolves over time, establishing constructive perspectives on the historical, social, and psychological forces that encourage so many women to develop eating issues (see Chapters 4, 5, and 6).

Personal exploration of feelings surrounding food and eating is encouraged through the use of food journals that members voluntarily share with the group each week. Members help one another analyze motives underlying personal behavior related to food, often drawing on parallel behavior in their own lives. Group exercises, utilizing simulation and role playing, generate new attitudes and behavior in relation to food. Sometimes homework will be given a particular individual; for example, asking a member whether she can request her spouse to sit with her one night a week at the table rather than always eating in front of the television. Occasionally, the group as a whole will undertake a homework assignment; for example, jointly visiting a health food store to explore alternative food sources.

Women in the group have the opportunity to modify cooking and eating behavior as a result of both food preparation and the actual sharing of the created meal. The therapist believes these latter segments of the weekly meeting are critically important if long-term behavioral change is to be effected. While preparing the evening's meal, the therapist initiates discussion of food sources, new ingredients, and cooking techniques. She also provides written menus and recipes weekly, utilizing flavorful and interesting whole foods that are low in fat and high in complex carbohydrates, in keeping with current FDA dietary guidelines. In this manner, group members over time accumulate nutritional resources based on the theoretical work of Colbin (1986), discussed in Chapter 7, and Jenkins (1992), discussed later in this chapter.

Not all women have an intrinsic interest in food or cooking when they first join Appetite for Change. Each woman does seem to realize at the time she joins the group, however, that she must take control of the food she eats as an important step in resolving her food issues. Preparation of the food she eats allows a woman to minimize many of the harmful chemicals present in prepared and processed food (see Chapters 4 and 5). She will be much more certain of the caloric and fat content of meals individually prepared with whole foods. Finally she can experiment with dietary changes that approximate a more balanced or "centered" nutritional pattern.

Food writers grounded in holistic nutrition (Colbin, 1986; Miller, 1979), have reaffirmed the author's own belief, based on personal experience, that a centered diet rich in complex carbohydrates is useful in reducing the cravings experienced by a compulsive eater or a bulimic woman who purges in a compulsive way. Because complex carbohydrates are converted into sugar rather slowly, the individual experiences a steady, extended period of energy for several hours after consumption of complex carbohydrates; they also do not create a sense of heaviness that often is associated with fat or protein consumption. Most grains and legumes are positioned near the center of the expansive/contractive food continuum (see Colbin discussion in Chapter 7) and, therefore, further reduce the body's tendency to crave oppositional food after eating food from either extreme of that continuum. The therapist actively supports any member's self-initiated efforts to smoke or drink less as an additional way to reduce cravings, since a body lurches from one extreme to the other in response to the stimulus of either nicotine or alcohol (Colbin, 1986).

Not Just a PC Version of Weight Watchers

Many diet programs, to their credit, now pay attention to the so-called yo-yo effect in dieting, whereby a body slows its metabolic rate when experiencing a sharp reduction in caloric intake (as in traditional diets); however, when the individual returns to her usual caloric intake level after achieving weight reduction goals, she quickly gains back those lost pounds, usually adding a few more in the process, because her body still metabolizes at the so-called starvation response level. Research has shown that diets dictating fewer than ten calories for each pound of weight induce this starvation response (Robb, 1989). In response, some dieting programs now recommend higher caloric levels in their diet instructions to avoid both the starvation response and its subsequent weight gain.

It could be argued theoretically that Appetite for Change really does not differ from some of the national dieting programs, especially ones that use behavior modification training in kitchens or lab kitchen settings.[2]

More recently, twelve-step programs (such as Overeaters Anonymous) designed for individuals experiencing problems with food have marketed an even more extreme concept: the notion that food must be regulated and controlled for a lifetime to overcome an eating disorder. The individual can never be trusted in an open relationship with food for the rest of her life.

The attraction of Appetite for Change for women who have had a lot of prior experience with programs based on weight reduction as a "body problem" is the integration of thought, emotion, and behavior possible around food issues via this approach.[3] Even though a compulsive eater, for example, feels food is her adversary in maintaining a particular body image during discussion earlier in the evening, during the cooking / eating experience that follows, she can reaffirm her positive interest in food and her enjoyment in eating a good meal in the company of caring women.

A woman joining Appetite for Change sometimes exhibits a "diet mentality," assuming she will be instructed in ways to modify her weight, and then be judged, as the weeks go by, on how successful she has been in making her body smaller. For such a woman, weight reduction is the only standard determining success or failure; this mental set encourages a passive view of the group process involved in Appetite for Change. This member waits, usually timidly, to be judged by the therapist and the other women in the group. Because she usually will not lose significant amounts of weight from week to week, this woman may feel guilty and worthless. Therefore she is not likely to express her opinions or make other contributions to the group. This woman has little appreciation of the need to explore underlying psychological issues related to food. She often is a patient listener for others, but feels she has little to contribute herself.

What such a woman often wants is a new diet to aid her in losing weight. The therapist is adamant that dieting ultimately will not help. Deprivation certainly is unnecessary and ultimately unhealthy. The therapist emphasizes that this member's activities in the kitchen are the means to permanent change in eating patterns. There she will learn new ways to prepare favorite foods, even "binge" food, so that what she eats contains fewer calories and significantly less fat. With this adjustment, enjoyable food can remain in the woman's diet without guilt or a sense of failure in her eating behavior. If a woman likes to eat loaf cake or fruit breads, for example, it is easy for her to reduce fat content without sacrificing flavor. This sort of information already is readily available in newspaper food sections and the popular press. But in the therapist's experience, it takes demonstrations with the actual foods a woman eats to make these adjustments realistic expectations: something the woman actually will try to accomplish.

The Group Experience

All eating disorders reflect strong urges or cravings for certain foods and patterns of eating. These cravings often manifest in oppositional behavior. Anorexia, for example, involves denying oneself food one so greatly craves, while compulsive eating allows one to act directly on that craving. It often is easier to identify others' psychological issues than to look inside ourselves. By having women with varied eating issues within one group, it is possible for a particular woman with, say bulimia, to acknowledge the triggers for another woman's compulsive eating binge even though she still may be unaware of the triggers for her own purging. In a similar fashion, a compulsive eater who usually cannot allow herself the same privileges other women have, may become more cognizant of her own self-denial when other group members point out instances in which she does not allow herself to be nurtured by food or other people.

It is easier to grasp the ways society encourages all women to develop self-destructive attitudes toward food when one can look beyond the reality of one's own particular "problem." As a result of more informal discussion around the dining table, members often reveal an expanded awareness of advertising and food marketing efforts that encourage alienation of a woman from the sensual and nurturant pleasures possible with food. While one group member may be railing against policies of the food industry, for instance, another member might be describing how good she felt making her own sun-dried tomatoes the past week.

It is important to clarify the ways in which a group focusing on *women's issues with food* differs from conventional group therapy for so-called eating disorders. The distinct experiences provided by the three segments of Appetite for Change weekly reinforce each other, perhaps in a symbiotic way. During the first part of the evening, the primary activity for the women involves *talking:* talking about members' actual food behavior since the last meeting, talking about strategies for change, and talking about the emotions attached to eating experiences. This is an important activity for several reasons: it serves as a catharsis for emotions related to eating issues, it creates a structure for a conceptualization of attitudes toward food, and it serves as a tool to help establish a mutually supportive environment for all group members as they strategize new approaches to old food issues. The latter half of each week's meeting, however, involves *action:* the preparation of the women's meal for that evening plus the actual experience of eating the meal together.

The juxtaposition of these two processes (talk and action) creates several possibilities for individual group members. Women who are articulate and comfortable talking about their food issues help less verbal group members to conceptualize their attitudes toward food. But these verbally facile members may be more proficient when talking about their problems than they are in actually changing their behavior toward food. So the challenge for these "talkers" may be actually adjusting their eating behavior to be more consistent with their thoughts about food and/or their intellectual understanding of their food problems. On the other hand, some group members either cannot or will not talk about their food issues much in group, but they will become very involved in the preparation of the group's meal; they might even engage in dyadic communication with another woman, say the one with whom they are chopping vegetables.

Eventually some feminist analysis is introduced by either the therapist or one of the group members. Not all women identify themselves as "feminist" when joining the group; but all members eventually understand the social and economic manipulations of women's relationship with food that constantly occurs in America. No woman is exempt from this unhealthy exposure. A group member might make negative comments about her own body, for example, when summarizing her food journal entries for the preceding week. Over time this same individual may come to realize the personal power generated by her refusal to acquiesce to the cultural expectation that all American women keep their bodies very small. She is expressing her refusal to acquiesce to society's demand that women keep their bodies very small in her own kitchen.

As previously mentioned, women join Appetite for Change with a wide variety of eating issues. Women experiencing different eating issues are intentionally grouped together because of the therapist's belief that all eating disorders have certain elements in common. For many women, disturbed eating has resulted in different eating disorders at various times in their lifetime; an anorexic young woman, for example, may become a compulsive eater at midlife.

As is common in any group of women with eating disorders, approximately two-thirds of the women in Appetite for Change have experienced sexual abuse in their lives. As discussed in the previous chapter, there is a strong link between the feeling of being "out of control" sexually and subsequent efforts to be "in control" of one's body through rigid control of the food one eats. As might be expected, sexual experiences in which a woman does not have personal control over the outcome of the event sometimes are recollected by a group member during the group process segment of the evening. These memories always are addressed by the therapist and, sometimes, also by other group members. For example, one member's presentation of previously repressed sexual abuse as a young teenager led to a group discussion of "weight as a protection against the advances of men."

A theme common to many of the women's eating experiences from week to week is their inability to nurture themselves either with food or some other means. The therapist finds she consistently must reinforce the *right* of a woman to food. It is common for group members to have been put on diets by their mothers at an early age. Some mothers even took their young daughters to "diet doctors" who prescribed amphetamines to curb youthful appetites. These individual realities coincide with research literature reports of this phenomenon in families regardless of race (Thompson, 1994). A larger woman in one group recollected how, throughout her childhood, she was denied any food between meals at home or generous portions of food at mealtimes. The rationale for this deprivation was that she already was "too big." This lead to her sneaking junk food bought at a convenience store on her way home from school each day. Over time this "eating on the sly" became the only way she nurtured herself, complete with lots of guilt and poor nutritional value in the food she was able to eat. So it was very important for the therapist and other group members to reassure this woman that she did, indeed, deserve to nurture herself. Perhaps there were other foods that could be used in this capacity? Perhaps there were things other than food that also could nurture this woman? Constructive questions like these can be used to encourage the woman's consideration of new attitudes and behavior.

What's for Dinner

After the group-process segment of the evening, the women prepare their evening meal in the therapist's kitchen. Each member gets a menu for that week's meal. Included are complete recipes for all the dishes served. Members are encouraged to save the weekly handouts in a loose-leaf notebook that becomes a "cookbook" of low-fat whole foods high in complex carbohydrates. This "hands on" experience in the kitchen seems to increase a woman's self-confidence in her own kitchen at home when she is totally responsible for the preparation of the food she eats. The women establish their internal group division of labor with different women making sauces, using the food processor, assembling a salad, creating a vinaigrette for that salad, setting the table, and arranging the foods to be eaten in an attractive and convenient manner.

That the therapist has created menus that are high in complex carbohydrates helps to smooth out the pendulum swing of blood sugar that accompanies many eating "binges" and food craving in general (see Colbin discussion in Chapter 7). Because of their low fat and caloric levels, complex carbohydrates can be eaten in greater amounts than simple sugars, proteins, and fats. Therefore the individual feels more psychologically and physiologically satisfied after a meal dominated by complex carbohydrates. An added bonus is that the digestion of carbohydrates uses more energy than metabolizing either protein or fat. So for a woman wishing to reduce body size over time, these high-complex-carbohydrate meals serve as an ideal way to accomplish this goal without reducing the volume of food eaten.

The emphasis on low fat foods in Appetite for Change is consistent with the finding that Americans generally eat more fatty foods than is good for their physical well being. For similar reasons, little salt and almost no simple sugars are included in the group's recipes. The therapist maintains a large herb garden that is utilized heavily in lieu of salt and sugar to "flavor" the foods eaten. The food eaten in Appetite for Change is nourishing with fewer calories than the food most women are eating before they enter the group. This diet coincides with the desire to reduce body size over time expressed by many group members. If, on the other hand, a woman is interested in gaining weight, the therapist points out ways to increase protein and fat levels in the recipes used by the group. Flexibility is important, since the differing needs of women require recipes that can be modified to satisfy individual requirements. The therapist also modifies the group's menus by season. Because we need different combinations of "expansive" and "contractive" foods in our diets depending on the season (Colbin, 1986), the therapist arranges the menus accordingly, emphasizing indigenous, seasonal foodstuffs (Jenkins, 1992), and periodically explains the adjustments she is making to group members during the food preparation segment of the evening.

The group's meals contain little, if any, meat, poultry, or fish. Partly, this is done because recommended protein levels do not require the massive hunks of meat Americans are used to eating. It also is beneficial to encourage women to explore alternative sources of protein, such as beans, lentils, and soy products, as substitutes for the meat and dairy usually associated with protein in America. An added advantage is that alternative sources of protein usually cost far less to buy in the food store and can serve as a useful demonstration that one can eat healthily at minimal cost. The therapist has an extensive personal collection of cookbooks and books about food. She often refers to particular books in discussions of menu, and lends books to group members upon request. The therapist believes that one aspect of her role as group facilitator is to encourage any behavior or activity that facilitates a woman taking active control of the food she eats.

It is important to emphasize the therapist's efforts to encourage the possibilities for having *fun* while cooking and eating each week.

There is so much personal pain expressed in the earlier part of the evening that the group needs levity and gaiety, sometimes bordering on silliness, as they work in the kitchen and eat together. The therapist is aware that a sense of playfulness also is a necessary precursor to the creative impulse. Creativity is called for, certainly, both when preparing food and resolving women's therapeutic issues.

Questions about the availability of ingredients and nutritional information are answered by the therapist during the course of the meal preparation and consumption each week. Over time, there is a tendency for group members to modify their daily diet, eating more complex carbohydrates in place of fats and protein, especially in meat, dairy, and processed food generally. Members often mention their efforts to duplicate dishes at home that were first eaten at Appetite for Change. A member's spontaneous comments about her efforts at home to modify group recipes to fit her own tastes and needs is an even better indicator that real dietary change is occurring.

The last hour of each week's group involves sitting together and eating the meal the group prepared. By the time group members actually sit down to eat, there usually are expressions of individuals' hunger in the air. A lot of energy and excitement surface at this time. The therapist has observed that, though careful to see that dishes are passed to all members, many of the women eat quickly, perhaps without tasting much of what is eaten. Therefore, she periodically will comment on the sensual pleasure of *feeling* the food in one's mouth while chewing it, or taking the time to *taste* the many different flavors in the food; attention to these sensory stimuli also is intended as a device for pacing eating. Chopsticks always are available, too, as another ploy, for western women at least, for extending the length of the activity of eating. Such devices are meant to increase the pleasure possible in the act of eating. It takes about twenty minutes for the stomach to know that it is full; therefore, eating more slowly allows that message to reach the brain before satiation has taken place. There always is plenty of food to eat with second helpings generally available. This strategy is intended to discourage fears of not getting enough to eat if the food is not quickly bolted down, a common concern among women with eating issues. The therapist encourages women to eat the amount of food that makes them comfortable, neither more nor less.

Conversation during meals varies considerably from week to week. Usually it is "light" while the group members are actually eating. At this point in the session, women still talk about food issues, but now the conversation is more informal and, therefore, more spontaneous. During mealtime, the group functions more as a "support" than a "therapy" group. Members might inquire, for example, about the results of one member's job interviews during the previous week. Topics like this are important events, but ones beyond the eating behavior parameters of the group.

But often after the women are through eating, they return to issues first introduced during the group therapy segment of the evening. Women now examine issues introduced earlier in the evening from a more dynamic, often assertive, perspective. There is more affirmation of themselves *as they are* and discussion of positive steps possible, rather than remaining "stuck" in previous patterns of behavior. It is as though the food has energized the women, and they now feel more confident and powerful in dealing with their individual problems.

WHAT AMERICANS EAT: FACT NOT FICTION

Chapters 4 and 5 discussed some of the ways class, regional, and ethnic differences affect eating behavior. Even though major differences exist among individuals, several trends have been identified in contemporary Americans' eating behavior. Many Americans now seek organically grown fruits and vegetables. About seven percent of the nation is said to be vegetarian. Most Americans, however persist in their old heavy-on-the-meat-and-dairy diet.[4]

Where are people eating all this food? Americans are eating out almost as much as they are eating at home. In 1993, six percent of total per capita income was spent in restaurants; only 7.2 percent, 1.2 percent more, was spent on food eaten at home. Eating out that same year, Americans had three-quarters of a million "eating places" in which they spent $276 billion (Mintz, 1996). One problem with food prepared outside the home is that the individual does not control, often does not even know, what ingredients and additives are in the food she consumes. The tendency to snack remains important in American eating habits. Eating a real meal at lunchtime is less likely, but the increased consumption of snacks during morning and afternoon breaks compensates for what is not eaten at noontime. It is obvious that Americans more and more are eating on the run.

Americans perceive themselves as never having enough time to complete all the important tasks they have in any given day. So the notion of convenience food, with its connotation of ready availability, appeals to people in a great hurry. Mintz (1996) has observed perceptively that "Americans are repeatedly told that they do not have enough time, I think because it serves to increase their aggregate consumption. Doing several things at once is touted as evidence of leadership; but what it does for the economy is to increase consumption" (p. 121).

As with anything else, not having the time to eat is a function of how much time is thought to be needed for other things. In my experience, most individuals grossly over-estimate the amount of time required to prepare an evening meal for themselves. Americans certainly would have more time to cook and to eat if they spent less time standing in supermarket lines, talking on the phone, driving in their cars, or watching television. Not only is time felt to be in short supply because there is so much to do, but also because Americans believe they already make good use of their time. Such notions about time allow for the great success of convenience food. But this sort of food also succeeds because most Americans care little about the quality and nutritional value of the food they eat. Some food anthropologists would go so far as to suggest there is no truly American cuisine because of Americans' disregard for what they put in their mouths (Mintz, 1996). This is an extreme notion, though eating without forethought does describe a disappointing, possibly dangerous, relationship with food. The following section describes alternative approaches to feeding ourselves that, if embraced by the American public, would stem further deterioration of current eating habits.

THE POLITICAL AS PERSONAL: VOTING WITH OUR FORKS

> A woman's body and her relationship to food is a paradigm for the use and control of food in the world. Just as food, a powerful tool, is used as punishment or reward within families (eat your spinach or you won't get dessert), on a larger scale, food policies are used as potent political weapons between and within nations. In the third world, women do more than consume food, they also produce the majority of the food in those countries. Yet these women have little control over its distribution and are thus impoverished as a direct result of their lack of power. Traditionally the last to eat, third world women get the least food, or are prohibited through food taboos from eating some of the most desirable (and nutritious) foods. (GB, 1987, p. 3)

If the personal is political in terms of understanding the relationship of eating issues to cultural forces promoting thinness, then the reverse also is true. By "the political is personal" I mean that, by altering our diet, it is possible to exercise some control over our food sources: to improve the health of our food supply and our very planet.

Farb and Armelagos (1980) have demonstrated mathematically that traditional methods of farming often produce more food for less energy. Foodways expert Jenkins (1992) has emphasized reconnection both with the food we eat and the earth that provides us with our food.[5] Jenkins has argued that contemporary ways of growing, harvesting, packaging, distributing, and cooking our food are not good for us or the world we live in. Not only are we exhausting the earth and destroying cultural connections to the earth, but we also are "missing out on one of the warmest and most enjoyable of human activities: the act of eating, the pleasures of the table" (p. 17).

Some say that nothing short of a national catastrophe will prompt us to graze lower on the food chain. Belasco has suggested that it will happen only when the world's population is forced by scarcity, which will come about because of environmentally produced shortages or economic collapse; "historically, that's been what's induced people to eat less" (Drexler, 1996, p. 29).

Just how badly are we exhausting the food supply in America?[6] A professor of Agricultural Sciences at Cornell University has direly projected that our food costs could multiply three to five times early in the twenty-first century. Americans now spend just 15 percent of their incomes on food, compared to 30 percent in European countries and 60 percent in Asia. So the average American possibly will be forced to eat more plant-based fare in the next century to keep food costs down. Because it takes less grain to produce chicken than beef, red meat consumption will be reduced dramatically because of price constraints. These predictions suggest that Americans will be eating a healthier diet, as defined by the American government, whether by individual choice or because of the increasingly expensive cost of reliance on animal products for nutrition.

Lappe (1971, 1977) has stated that the very act of eating involves one in agriculture. Most Americans do not know, or care to know, how dependent their food supply is on fertilizers, pesticides, herbicides, growth regulators, and genetically engineered plants and animals, all necessary, we are told, to keep the bumper crops coming to feed people in our own country and to export to hungry nations. We have been told these agricultural practices must be continued to sustain our food supply; but Jenkins (1992) has argued that "sustainable agriculture" is poisoning our water supply, eroding our topsoil, and dissipating plant diversity. Jenkins has maintained that, contrary to many Americans' belief that they are eating less meat these days, meat consumption has never been higher.[7]

International trade agreements increasingly allow our food to be imported from ever-greater distances. Now there is even less control over the conditions under which the food is raised and shipped. What additional preservatives, for example, are required to keep raspberries from rotting on their trip from Chile to Boston? The energy waste in the cost of intercontinental food transportation is greater than the already huge expenditure of energy by American agribusiness at the end of the century.

Awareness of these realities could cause an individual to feel she has no choice in the matter, that the production of food is totally out of her control. But Jenkins (1992) has argued that we *do* have choices and we *can* exercise control: "like sheep grazing in toxic pastures, we have become a herd of passive and uncritical eaters" (p. 17). We can make "kitchen-counter reforms," a phrase coined by the World-watch Institute, a Washington think tank, to describe dietary changes that can influence policy and practice in the production and provision of food around the globe. Jenkins has used the phrase, "voting with your fork," to remind Americans that by eating indigenous, organic, fresh, seasonal food and consuming less meat, if possible, they can have a positive impact on food production in America and around the world.[8] Upon reflection, Jenkins has provided an addendum to her four cardinal rules of eating; one also should take time to think about preparing well what foodstuffs you obtain in this fashion:

> Selecting food wisely, eating with consciousness, eating with gratitude for the products on the table and for the skills of the farmer and the cook, is not elitist. . . . Among life's greatest pleasures, after all, are those moments when strangers become friends and friends become lovers; when families become, in the fullest and richest sense, families; and when memories, strong, intense and persistent, are given birth. (p. 19)

It has been suggested that "western feminism is an oppositional subculture and requires an Other with whom it does not share experience. Creating an Other whom one can oppose is a form of power relations that feminists engage in unwittingly" (hooks, 1994). This sardonic observation could refer to American women's dominant role in world hunger campaigns (see Chapters 4 and 5); in many ways it is easier to focus on world hunger than to consider the hunger existing within American borders.

As of 1993, for example, a record 27.4 million people, approximately 10 percent of the American population and nine million more than the total for 1989, were receiving food stamps (Clarke, 1993). Furthermore, Bread for the World, a Washington-based international, interfaith policy agency, has estimated that one American child in four is growing up hungry. These numbers have been swollen by the country's nouveau poor: recently laid-off workers; "permanent part-time" workers, and industrial workers who now must take jobs that offer a fraction of their previous salaries. The consciences of those with full bellies are assuaged by the existence of the 50,000 private food banks and pantries throughout the United States. Actually only 52 percent of the people whose income makes them eligible for food stamps have been receiving them. Ironically, for every dollar spent to feed a hungry mother or child, the American government could save the four dollars it spends on costs related to the health problems of low-birth-weight infants and malnourished children at the close of the century.

What better way to help resolve this half-hidden American tragedy than to donate the money saved by following Jenkins' mantra to eat only indigenous, fresh, local, seasonal food; savings could be donated to a local food bank for the benefit of those who do not have the luxury of this option.

Conclusions

THE "PIG IN THE PYTHON" REACHES THE GUT[1]

I believe that the aging American population has initiated at least two positive trends. When yuppies broke age fifty, we began seeing some encouraging signs of a greater cultural acceptance of full-figured women. Cultural tolerance for larger women trickled forth: the appearance of "special size" shops for women's clothing and a token sprinkling of larger size media models during the latter 1990s. A second effect of the "graying of America" has resulted in nutrition once again re-emerging as an active focus for Americans, especially older ones; this time nutrition has been constructed as a means to better health and *longevity*. Both cultural trends suggest that Americans may be more receptive, though perhaps for different reasons, to Jenkins' suggestions for responsible eating as summarized in the previous chapter.

YOU ARE WHAT YOU EAT

Regardless of motivation, any reduction in the prevalent late-twentieth century assumption that the American consumer is entitled to all foodstuffs, regardless of cost, at any time of the year, concomitantly would reduce pressure on subsistence farmers to sacrifice valuable growing space so as to produce cash crops for export to wealthy industrialized nations. Awareness of this situation on the part of affluent American consumers just might force consideration of the quintessential question: do the ends justify the means?

At the same time Mintz' (1996) observations of America's eating behavior at the end of the century (discussed in Chapter 8) are unsettling; they suggest that America's dominant dietary patterns are very conducive to the yin-yang swings we already have identified as antecedents of food cravings and other manifestations of an out-of-control relationship with food (see Chapter 7).

I believe the outcome is a toss-up. Whether privileged Americans' preference for locally grown, organic, seasonal foodstuffs becomes affordable for Americans of more average means will determine the outcome of what otherwise will be a predictable (and socially un-conscionable) emulation of the rich by the middle class.

Dietary improvements also could be facilitated by public service advertisements in the mass media, perhaps modeled after those successfully broadcasting the dangers of smoking over the airwaves during the last decade of the twentieth century. In this scenario, the currently ambiguous attitudes most Americans' manifest in relation to food would be dealt with in an optimistic manner: a belief that all individuals truly want to eat well to maximize their good health over a lifetime. This sort of public advertising campaign would need to make the connection between current eating behavior and the individual's expectations for future health over and over again; perhaps "you are what you eat" could be used as their slogan. The anti-smoking media campaign again serves as a model for soldering this connection (current diet = future health) in the minds of the masses.

I believe it is much easier to work for dietary change at an earlier age. Chapter 2 provided many illustrations of the importance of dietary associations made early in life. If home and school environments were to expose children to a wholesome diet of whole foods that also were kind to the earth from an early age, children most likely would demonstrate a proclivity for these foods long past their formative years.[2]

Again an analogy from the mass media. It is impressive to consider how much the last generation or two of Americans, especially when compared with their grandparents' generation, register more sympathetic attitudes toward wildlife and the habitats necessary for these animals' existence. I believe that early exposure to "nature programs" on television, including "Wild Kingdom" and all its descendants over the past thirty years, is largely responsible for these favorable attitudes toward the preservation of "nature" in America at the start of the twenty-first century. A similar likelihood of empathy for the world's majority of subsistence farmers perhaps could be fostered via a favorable public relations campaign that made the relationship between our food preferences here in America and the health of those people who have been deemed the providers of American foodstuffs, whether or not they want to take on that role.

DO THE ENDS JUSTIFY THE MEANS?

It was Lappe (1971, 1977) who originally made the insightful observation that telling kids about "the poor starving kids in . . ." as a ploy for the clean plate club actually began a desensitization process to world hunger at a very early age. In this way, Americans can remain largely guilt free about the effects of the first world's overuse of the planet's resources to the detriment of the food supply of all the world's people. Television programming that was factually honest about the impact of hybridized seeds, energy-guzzling equipment, fertilizers, pesticides, expensive air transport, and other modern-day farming procedures that can be obtained only with "hard" western currency would be a useful beginning. It also would be helpful to educate American youth about the monetary profits these procedures yield for a small group of first world capitalists at the expense of world citizens in poorer nations who now have sacrificed scarce land resources to grow cash crops the high-tech way so that their mother countries can earn the foreign currency credit required to pay for all this western technology. It is a double no-win situation for the little guys; they lose valuable subsistence crop land to extravagant farm crops they themselves will never eat.

My interpretation of world hunger is very different from the currently fashionable notion that "overpopulation" of the planet is the culprit. But the television programming I envision could result in an awareness that individual citizens of the first world also are implicated in the world hunger crisis and, therefore, have the option to do something in a direct, personal manner to improve the chances that all living beings can get enough to eat each day.

BRINGING "OTHER" IN FROM THE MARGINS[3]

To be in the margin is to be part of the whole but outside the main body.
(hooks, 1984, p. ix)

One of the advantages of this vantage point is one's unique perception, or "world view," when sitting on the outside observing the activities within; it is much easier to analyze what's going on from the outside. For purposes of this volume, however, I have assumed that most American women would rather be participants than observers.

The evolution of women's relationships with food from an earlier stance that conferred individual power and self-esteem to women already has been documented in Chapters 2 and 3. When human beings evolved from horticultural to agrarian societies, females experienced a steep reduction in status and personal power with the new division of labor. The evolution of industrialized society, however, really solidified women's position as second-class citizens; females now were seen not only as "possessions" of dominant males, but, in America at least, the industrial revolution dissolved their perceived worthiness as food producers, preparers, and processors. This outcome encouraged negative feelings about self: a perfect setup for eating disturbances that have seemed to increasingly blossom over the decades of the twentieth century.

Ultimately, an analysis of women's relationships with food requires a feminist interpretation of the events leading to the explosion of women's illnesses associated with food and body image at the close of the twentieth century. Feminism already has taught us that women can heal themselves if they regain some sense of personal worth and control in their lives. These qualities have been muted for many western women over a span of several centuries. Twentieth-century feminism, however, has provided a working space for American women to regain the qualities required to once again become healthy, whole individuals.

In this manner, women as "other" in today's misogynous American society will move in from the margins only when it is possible to be part of an androgynous society where both sexes seek new definitions of "masculine" and "feminine." Women then will be at rest, centered at last in a society committed to the equitable treatment of all individuals. This analysis of women's relationship with food was intended to do just that!

Notes

CHAPTER ONE,
FOOD IS EVERYONE'S FIRST LANGUAGE, pp. 1–10

1. The author first heard the above phrase in film maker Paul Kwan's wonderful food memoir, *Anatomy of a Spring Roll*.

2. A pregnant or lactating woman has a walking radius of only a few miles a day. Therefore, since only females could give birth and provide nourishment for newborns from their bodies, it was logical for pre-Homo sapiens females to develop skill in gathering the foodstuffs that were available near the group's campsite; they also provided childcare and physically maintained the base camp. Pre-Homo sapiens males, on the other hand, were left to develop hunting skills and to provide protection for the females and young in their group.

3. A recent cover story in a major national magazine of natural phenomena reported the startling results of ongoing archaeological research centered around the Ice Age settlement of present-day Dolni Vestonice in the Czech Republic (Pringle, 1998). Not only have these remains reinforced the currently widespread belief that females contributed the bulk of the food supply in early hunter-gatherer societies, but these new analyses of 26,000-year-old remains strongly suggest that women also were regular providers of animal protein for their Ice Age settlements. Using a zoom stereomicroscope, archaeologists discovered evidence of the use of cordage mesh nets by females to trap smaller animals (deer, giant hare, and fox) who then could easily be beaten to death by any adult female. Furthermore, some archaeologists believe that Venus figurines found at this and other Ice Age settlement sites suggest that women may have been principal players in spiritual rituals used to invoke a good hunt.

4. Chapters 2 and 3 serve this purpose. An anthropological clarification of the evolution of social sex role is necessary to comprehend the importance of women's traditional role in relationship to food. Chapter 2 will detail the changes in a sexual division of labor that accompanied the evolution of new ways to organize society. Chapter 3 will discuss the enormous influence the industrial revolution had on women's relationship to food in American society: from processed food to the application of scientific principles in all aspects of domesticity.

5. This phrase is the axiom of Oldways Preservation and Exchange Trust, a Boston-based non-profit organization until recently directed by Nancy Harmon Jenkins, that seeks to educate people about traditional ways of dealing with food.

CHAPTER TWO,
WOMAN THE PROVIDER, pp. 11–39

1. This volume uses the terms "foraging" and "hunting-gathering" interchangeably when describing the oldest known human societies.

2. One of the remarkable discoveries of Jane Van Lawick Goodall in her years of research on chimpanzees in the Gombe National Park in Tanzania was that chimpanzees "fished" for termites. This involved breaking off a twig, stripping it of leaves and side branches, and then inserting it into an underground termite nest and extracting the twig with its clinging termites (Goodall, 1973).

3. For example, female chimpanzees fish for termites over three times as frequently as males. In contrast, male chimpanzees predominate in the use of weapons and projectiles (McGrew, 1981; Goodall, 1968).

4. Hunting and gathering as a way of life has virtually disappeared in the contemporary world, not because it was not viable, but because of the encroachments of technogically more advanced peoples onto their land, from Neolithic farmers and herders, to more recent Euro-American colonialists. Those who managed to survive contact and maintain a traditional life now exist only in the most remote regions of the world. Existing sites are not representative of the range of habitats and cultural adaptations in times past. One needs to be extremely cautious, therefore, in reconstructing the history of foraging peoples. The fact that anthropologists have found that contemporary hunters and gatherers, even those in marginal environments, have abundant, varied, and nutritious food, and a relatively secure way of life challenges prevalent anthropological opinion that the way of lives of prehistoric foragers was precarious and full of hardship.

5. Draper (1975), for example, has commented on the self-esteem !Kung women derive from from their contribution to subsistence: "!Kung women agree that meat is the most desirable, most prestigious food, but the hunter cannot always provide it. Without question, women derive self-esteem from the regular daily contribution they make to the family's food" (p. 82).

Draper also has reported that these women are skilled in reading the signs of the bush, taking careful note of the animal tracks and direction of movement. Men generally use women's reconnaissance to gain valuable information about game movements and the location of water.

6. Draper (1975), comparing contemporary !Kung women in foraging and sedentary contexts, has found that village women do most of the cooking, drying, and storing of foodstuffs.

> Homebound, their hands are busier, and their time is taken up with domestic chores . . . under settled conditions food preparation is more complicated, although the actual diet is probably less varied in comparison with that of the foragers. Grains and squash must be brought in from the fields and set up on racks to dry. Sorghum and corn are pounded into meal; squash and melons are peeled and then boiled before eating. (p. 101)

In a similar manner, early horticultural women must have worked harder as compared to their foraging sisters.

Another comtemporary analogue is provided by the Bemba of Zambia, where the women work with the men in the fields, cultivating millet and other crops. Women also brew beer, an item essential for hospitality and special occasions. The preparation of a batch of beer takes between four and seven days of intermittent activity. Additionally, women are the food processors; they also gather firewood and fetch water for all their cooking and brewing. The preparation of porridge, a staple at each meal, requires two or three hours of threshing and pounding grain every day. The fact that women alone collect bush foods and harvest subsidiary crops used for side dishes gives them control over how much food will be prepared for the daily meals; any day a woman is too tired or busy to collect relishes, she simply does not cook (Richards, 1939).

7. By comparison, only 10 percent of hunting-gathering societies, four percent of agrarian societies, and virtually no industrial societies practice

matrilineality, whereas 26 percent of horticultural societies are matrilineal (Lenski and Lenski, 1978).

8. Strathern (1972) has written persuasively about the serene, fulfilling lives of Hagen women in New Guinea:

> Constant concern with the minutiae of food production produces an emotional involvement. The refrains of women's songs hark on themes relating to their garden work. Accounts by some of how their time is spent comprise detailed catalogues of all the crops they grow, and all the names of all the varieties, how they plant them, dig them up, cook them and then share them out.... Gardens are probably of greater importance to women than they are to men. They spend long hours working there, and the pigs they care for have to be fed with garden produce. Women are sensitive about their control over crops. It is in the disposal of foodstuffs that they can demonstrate generosity. The popular woman is one always ready to feed visitors who come to her house, and to invite neighbours to any special food cooking she holds. (p. 134)

9. With the innovation and spread of intensive cultivation techniques: "women dropped out of the mainstream of production for the first time in the history of cultural evolution. The consequence of this reversal in economic roles permeated every corner of their social experience" (Martin & Voohries, 1975, p. 290).

10. Despite vast social change and the expansion of empires from the fifteenth to eighteenth centuries, the lives of women seemed relatively unchanged. Miles (1988) has commented perceptively:

> Throughout all this women everywhere tended their children, milked their cattle, tilled their fields, washed, baked, cleaned and sewed, healed the sick, sat by the dying and laid out the dead—just as at this moment some women, somewhere are doing to this day. The extraordinary continuity of women's work from country to country and age to age, is one of the reasons for its invisibility. (p. 122)

11. In fact, this reliance on women's labor producing corn in 1728 Virginia prompted William Byrd to write, "Indian corn is of so great increase, that a little Pains will subsist a very large Family with Bread.... The men, for their Parts, just like the Indians, impose all the Work upon the poor Women. They make their Wives rise out of their Beds early in the Morning, at the same time that they Lye and Snore" (Hardeman, 1981, p. 37).

12. An acre or so of improved land near the house usually was set aside for the domestic garden, consistent with the English tradition delineating a woman's environment as the garden, the family dwelling, plus any surrounding structures, which included cellars, pantries, brewhouses, butteries, and milkhouses (Ulrich, 1991). For two centuries, virtually everything that a colonial housewife's family used or ate was produced at home under her direction: she brought fruits and vegetables, dairy, poultry, and cured meat to the table; she spun and dyed the yarn that she then wove into cloth, and cut and hand-stitched into garments; she grew much of the food her family ate, preserving enough to last the winter months; she made butter, cheese, bread, candles, and soap, and even knitted her family's stockings (Wertheimer, 1977).

13. A preference for wheat was evident in this Kansan frontier woman's recollections:

> Our living at first was very scanty, mostly corn coarsely ground or made into hominy. After we had raised a crop of wheat and had some ground, we would invite the neighbors, proudly telling them we would have "flour doings." Next it was "chicken fixings." And when we could have "flour doings and chicken fixins" at the same meal we felt we were on the road to prosperity. (Stratton, 1981, p. 63)

In contrast, a Native American woman described raising corn around the turn of the century in the Dakotas:

> We cared for our corn in those days, as we would care for a child; for we Indian people loved our fields as mothers love their children. We thought that the corn plants had souls as children have souls and that the growing corn liked to hear us sing, as children like to hear their mothers sing to them. (Jensen, 1986, p. 21)

14. Ulrich (1991) has described the varied activities of housewives in the coastal towns and villages:

> Trading for food might require as much energy and skill as manufacturing or growing it. One key to success was simply knowing where to go. Keeping abreast of the arrival of ships in the harbor or establishing personal contact with just the right farmwife from nearby Salem village required time and attention. Equally important was the ability to evaluate the variety of unstandardized goods offered. An apparently sound cheese might teem with maggots when cut. . . . Petty haggling over direct exchanges was also a feature of this barter economy. (p. 47)

In this they were not very different from peasant women elsewhere or, for that matter, from African horticultural women who routinely market their domestic surpluses. An exerpt from Faragher's (1991) account of an 1850s midwestern farm family has provided yet another example of the continued importance of women's extra-domestic distribution and exchange:

> The products of dairy, henhouse, garden, and loom were often the only commodities successfully exchanged for other family necessities. Powder, glass, dyes, crockery, coffee, tea, store cloth, metal utensils and sugar

> were bought on credit from the local merchant; butter, cheese, eggs, vege-
> tables, homespun and whiskey were the main items offered in trade to pay
> the tab. (p. 129)

15. One example of this mind set occurred in the distant peasant village
of Colpied in southern France, where it was claimed that women did not
work, although they spent many hours every day caring for house and
family. They also raised the chickens and rabbits, and worked in the fields
during critical periods. All women claimed to hate agricultural work and
to know nothing about it (as opposed to men who were the specialists).
But most cut lavender every summer, and in the fall they harvested
grapes, both tasks not considered "work" by either sex (Reiter, 1975).

CHAPTER THREE,
SUBVERSION BY FOOD PROCESSORS AND
REFORMERS, pp. 41–59

1. Levenstein (1988) coined the term "giant food processors" in his vision-
ary account of the transformation of food production and consumption
that was triggered by the industrial revolution. In a nutshell,

> The rise of the giant processors marked the beginning of a momentous
> change in the history of food and diet, not just in America but in the world.
> Throughout human history food has been a primary item for exchange,
> barter, and sale, and people have amassed wealth by doing so. Wars have
> been fought and empires have risen and fallen in struggles for control of
> food supplies. But the fortunes and the struggles have arisen on the as-
> sumption that there was an existing market for the items involved,
> whether it was spices of the Orient, the fisheries of the North Sea and
> North Atlantic, or the sugar of the West Indies. . . . Using new methods of
> capital formation to raise money for the technology of mass production,
> new organizational techniques to integrate their operations vertically, and
> new promotional methods as well as sheer size to market their products
> on a mass basis, these giants were now able to struggle against their great-
> est enemy, the forces of the uncontrolled marketplace. They now aspired
> not only to respond to consumer demands but to shape them. (pp. 42–43)

2. On the basis of her own food oral history research, the author would
add that rural American-born housewives also continued this hot summer work well into the twentieth century. They were likely to make negative comments about more affluent women's tendency to buy canned
food in the grocery store rather than home canning their family's winter
produce. Visitors to these rural households might even be shown special
closets or basement rooms constructed to house shelf upon shelf of Mason
or Ball jars displaying the bounty of the previous summer's harvest.

Levenstein (1988) has made a similar observation about foreign-born women in his vivid description of one such immigrant's report, originally made in 1907:

> Foreign-born people used to make disparaging remarks about native American women sitting in the shade in the summer heat fanning themselves while the foreign-born women sweated in their kitchens putting up hundreds of jars of beans, tomatoes, preserves, jellies, pickles, beets, fruits of all kinds. Instead of putting up vegetables, meat etc., for the winter native Americans bought canned goods from the store. None of the foreign-born women would be caught dead with store bread on the table. (p. 107)

3. Levenstein has used the term "new nutritionists" to refer to the food reformers who flourished in this country after the initial success of the Boston Cooking School, founded in 1879. Shapiro has used the term "domestic scientists" for these same reformers. The author uses the more general term "food reformers" unless specifically referring to Levenstein's or Shapiro's research; in such instances, the author's preferred term is used.

4. Disconnection from the past and guilt instilled by domestic science regarding the average woman's ability to cook and adequately care for her family can clearly be felt in Shapiro's concluding remarks regarding home economists' progress during the early decades of the twentieth century: "Mother's cooking, the old-fashioned country kitchen, the groaning board laden with mince pies—all these familiar symbols of well-being were to them symbols of degeneracy, and the women confined to such a past were doomed" (1986, p. 190).

5. The disdain food reformers felt towards food actually eaten and the manner in which it was prepared is very evident in the following passage from Levenstein's discussion of reformers and immigrants.

> Their narrowness stemmed from their determination to learn only from science and not from the accumulated experience of millions of Europeans forced to economize on food. Nutritional science told them that the essence of European economical cooking: the *minestras* and *pasta-fagioles* of Italy, the *borschts*, *gulyashen*, and *cholents* of Eastern Europe were uneconomical because they were mixtures of foods and therefore required uneconomical expenditures of energy to digest. Strong seasonings that made bland but cheap foods tasty were denounced for overworking the digestive process and stimulating cravings for alcohol. Nutritional science reinforced what their palates and stomachs already told them: that any cuisine as coarse, overspiced, "garlicky," and indelicate-looking as the food of central, eastern, and southern Europe must be unhealthy as well. To most of these native-born daughters of the middle and upper class, who preferred their own food awash in a sea of bland white sauce and for whom

"dainty" was the greatest compliment one could bestow on food, one whiff of the pungent air in the tenements or a glance into the stew pots was enough to confirm that the contents must wreak havoc on the human digestive system. (1988, pp. 103–104)

Imagine the powerful effect such attitudes could have on immigrant women trying to find their way in a new culture. Not only would they not be serving their family's best interests by clinging to the food of the "old country," but these traditional housewives also would be delaying their family's assimilation into the culture of their new country since "food preferences often became the touchstone of Americanization" (Levenstein, 1988, p. 105).

6. Housewives from middle and eastern European cultures would challenge Levenstein's assumption that their foods are "less sophisticated." Rather these cuisines tended to be based on a smaller number of traditionally available foodstuffs and, therefore, might be more readily abandoned, or expanded, when a greater array of basic food resources became available.

7. Even though some groups remained resistant to such a message, Levenstein (1988) has suggested that at least the children received the message loud and clear: "The children may have remained chained to their mothers' cuisine, but they were learning an important lesson: it was the food in their homes, not on the steam tables, which was out of the main stream, and that to enter that stream they would ultimately have to learn to appreciate its food" (p. 119).

8. The following passage from ad copy in turn of the century issues of *Ladies Home Journal* serves as an excellent early example of advertising designed to make women question their "natural" or innate feminine qualities: in this case their ability to adequately feed their children in their early years of life.

The mammary glands have suffered . . . outrages at the hands of corsetmaker, the dressmaker, and the manufacturer of bosom pads, so that what is left of our mothers is in the majority of cases only an apology for the ideal which nature designed. . . . In all classes and conditions of modern life, the mother's milk is most frequently neither in quantity nor quality adequate to the nourishment of the child. . . . BUT THE BANE HAS AN ANTIDOTE. (Levenstein, 1988, p. 123)

9. All elements of this conundrum are reflected in the following ad copy for "Cocomalt" in a 1928 issue of *Good Housekeeping:*

So many things you do for them, . . . which will count most in the years to come. . . . So many little garments to be mended . . . so many childish faults to overcome . . . so many difficulties to be smoothed away. . . . How you work and plan for them, those children of yours—how *much* you try to do!

> But most of all you think about safeguarding their health. . . . Like most
> modern mothers you know a great deal about the essential elements of the
> well-balanced diet. You know how valuable a food is milk. (Levenstein,
> 1988, pp.154–55)

It is likely that many "modern" mothers reading this ad did *not* feel they actually knew a great deal about nutrition and, so, were easily convinced to
let "Cocomalt" experts instruct them in the proper feeding of their children.

10. The feedback from many food oral histories of women from various
ethnic / racial backgrounds has been that use of Betty Crocker's recipes is
still considered a cultural "step up" for housewives eager to join mainstream American culture.

11. Levenstein (1988) has included a devastating example of this effort to
get all Americans eating Anglo cuisine, what he refers to as "Americanization through Homemaking," in his description of the tyranny of a home
economics classroom in southern California designed to teach Mexican-
American girls both homemaking and citizenship:

> Its director warned that malnourishment not only led Mexicans into lives
> of thievery but it also contributed to revolutionary tendencies. It was
> therefore necessary to teach them the basics of the New and Newer Nutri-
> tions in the Anglo-Saxon cooking manner. A prime objective was to con-
> vince them to abandon the traditional Mexican sauces (whose tomatoes
> and chiles provided vitamins and whose nuts and cheese provided pro-
> tein, calcium, and vitamins), in favor of only two sauces: White Sauce, con-
> sisting of flour, butter and milk, and Hard Sauce, mainly sugar and butter.
> (p. 157)

Shapiro (1986) has given an equally devastating example from her own
experience in home economics class: one that suggests the pervasiveness
of exclusionary views across time, social class, and geographical location:

> I have only made carrot-and-raisin salad once, the day it was taught to me
> in the seventh grade, but the memory of those bright orange shreds
> specked with raisins and clotted with mayonnaise has been unaccounta-
> bly hard to shake. It's easy to understand why the recipe appealed to the
> teacher—carrots made it nutritious, raisins made it sweet, and mayon-
> naise made it a salad—but I can't explain why a combination I never
> hoped to eat again was able to lodge itself so firmly into the apparatus of
> my adolescence. Perhaps those endless Wednesday-afternoon classes,
> known in 1958 as "Homemaking," had a grip on us that we hardly sus-
> pected at the time, codifying as they did a grim and witless set of expecta-
> tions that loomed across the future like a ten commandments for girls.
> Eerily enough, this course, which purported to be about the real world,
> had nothing whatever to do with anything that happened in my home or
> that I had ever seen happen anywhere else. Why were they claiming life
> was like this? Who on earth wore pink cotton "hostess aprons" or, worse
> yet, had to sew them? None of us knew enough to rebel in those days, but

the sheer emptiness at the core of home economics was stunning, if not within the reach of consciousness just then. (pp. 217–18)

Teaching of this sort illustrated how misogyny and ethnic/racial prejudice went hand-in-hand with efforts to standardize women's behavior; which coincidentally also made it easier to sell food products in a mass market.

12. Levenstein (1988) has documented the pressures this new cultural ideal created for middle-class women.

Had these new styles merely affected single girls on the marriage market, the effect on food habits would have been negligible. In earlier times it was not unheard of for women to starve themselves until marriage and then abandon all concern over bulging bodies as they enjoyed the pleasures of the family, the table, and the sweet shop. But the heightened sexual expectations of middle-class marriage meant that married women now had to engage in a two-front battle against aging (for youthfulness in women was still regarded as sexually attractive) and weight. (p. 165)

13.

Of necessity, these women were proud of their *lifeless palates*. The *naked* act of eating was little more than unavoidable, as far as gently raised women of their era were concerned, and was *not to be considered a pleasure* except with great discretion. Domestic scientists were inspired by the nutritive properties of food, by its ability to promote physical, social, and, they believed, moral growth. The flavors of food were of slight, somewhat anthropological interest. They did understand very well that many people enjoyed eating; this presented still another *challenge. Food was powerful*, it could draw forth *cravings* and *greedy desires* which had to be *met with a firm hand.* Their goal as a group was to transubstantiate food, and it didn't matter a great deal whether the preferred method was to reduce a dish to its simplest components or to blanket it with whipped cream and candied violets. *Containing and controlling food, draining it of taste and texture* . . . these were some of the major culinary themes of the domestic-science movement. (Shapiro, 1986, pp. 6–7; italics added)

This language is remarkably similar to that of contemporary women struggling with their own issues with food. It is the language of eating disorders.

14. *People* magazine (Too fat?, 1996), for example, devoted a cover story to the issue of how media images of celebrities teach kids to hate their bodies.

15. In her radical feminist analysis of twentieth-century architectural styles, Wajcman (1991) has meticulously enumerated the ways in which a home's interior design reflected housewives' alienation in the suburbs after World War II:

For women, the machine was to become a treadmill. The kitchen, now de-signed for the servantless family, was a compact fitted kitchen with room for one worker, the housewife. Neither its small size nor its location, sealed off from the rest of the house, were conducive to the sharing of kitchen du-ties. . . . This model was to become the prototype for working-class as well as middle-class homes. (p. 114)

CHAPTER FOUR,
MORAL MANIPULATION, pp. 61–73

1. In Belasco's own lively words, "Living lightly meant keeping loose, open, young in spirit, yet also staying close to the earth, humble, classi-cally conservative. To be 'heavy' was to be weighed down not so much by pounds of flesh as by the burdensome attachments of middle-class culture and middle age" (1989, p. 225).

2. One meaning of the actual counterculture nudity that got lost in this commercial translation was hippie awareness that "weight control did have some underground context: an ascetic badge of living lightly, a rejec-tion of bloated affluence, a tool of self-discipline, a way to train for the struggle ahead" (p. 178).

3. Marion Nestle, chair of the Department of Nutrition and Food Studies at New York University, has nicely summed up this collusion: "I'd like to see government policies that foster consumption of fruits, vegetables, and grains in the same way they currently foster consumption of meat and dairy products" (Drexler, 1996, p. 27).

4. Belasco (1989) has reported that a 1960s People's Park teach-in pam-phlet, for example, included a poem by Book Jones that dramatically ex-pressed the harsh notion that pollution endangering the earth was analogous to a woman being raped:

> The earth is our Mother the land
> The University put a fence around the land—our Mother
> The University must stop fucking with our land
> The University must stop being a Motherfucker. (p. 34)

5. Belasco (1989) reviewed the 1970 edition of *Our Bodies, Ourselves*, and found that this enormously successful "self health" manual written by the Boston Women's Collective stated, "We want to become physically healthy and strong and enduring, through exercise, proper eating, and training (like karate) and proud of ourselves, proud because we feel good about ourselves, not because we look good for others" (p. 36).

6. As Roberta Weintraub wrote for *Liberation News Service*, "Fat is a defense against men, but it is also a major source of conflict and unhappiness in women" (Belasco, 1989, p. 35).

7. With stunning cynicism, Belasco (1989) has summarized a lot of the psychology that made communal living seem so attractive:

> What better way to find nature than to move to the country? What better way to identify with brown-skinned peasants than to live in a peasant village oneself? What better way to experience organic interrelatedness than to live in a tribe where everyone spoke the same deviant language. (p. 76)

8. As Lappe (1971) described this happy encounter, "I remember devouring my first 'natural goods' cookbook as if it were a novel. Barley, mushrooms, and dill together? Cheddar cheese, walnuts, and rice? How odd. What would that taste like?" (Belasco, 1989, pp. 45–46).

CHAPTER FIVE, THE MORE WE CHANGE, THE MORE WE STAY THE SAME, pp. 75–85

1. Mintz (1996) has reported that in 1994 a national market research group compiled a list of ten favorite lunch and dinner "entrees." The list began with pizza, ham sandwiches, and hot dogs and ended with cheese sandwiches, hamburger sandwiches, and spaghetti. Mintz' conclusion? "I don't think anyone wants to call that array a cuisine" (p. 114). Mintz has stated that a cuisine can exist only if "there is a community of people who eat it, cook it, have opinions about it, and engage in dialogue involving those opinions" (p. 117).

2. Some food researchers have suggested that recent appreciation of gourmet food in America actually might be a permanent phenomenon. Shapiro (1986) has stated that, even when the element of fad and fashion are discounted, "the common denominators of American taste may well have changed permanently" (p. 230). O'Neill (1998) has emphasized the speed of culinary assimilation at the end of the twentieth century:

> In the past, when fate, conquest or immigration threw disparate cultures together, their cuisines would circle each other like cats. Each would flaunt its appearance and obvious attributes. And over time, they might form a nodding acquaintance. But it could take generations, sometimes centuries, before they would share each other's cooking secrets. (p. 47)

During the last two decades of the century, however, culinary assimilation has quickened at a breathtaking pace. The world has shrunk to a point where, for example, popular Malaysian cuisine one year is replaced by an intense interest in Cuban cooking the next. And each cuisine, first popular in restaurants, quickly develops the potential for an appearance at dinner time in mainstream America since critical ingredients rapidly appear on the shelves of the local supermarket.

3. Meloy (1993) has described this tendency in blunt terms:

> The gourmet fetishism of the 1980s turned us into food snobs. There is nothing new about this condition . . . except for its irony. Organ meats, edible flowers, blood sausage, and the like, once the fare of the poor, now sizzle the palates of the affluent, who scorn cheap mainstream baloney, irradiated fruit, Dweemo, Spam, pink sugar, and other processed foods containing oil-based flavors we fought Iraq for. To irony, add the illusion that we can live off the land, eat food close to the source. Not too many people remember what the source is. Not much of either the source or the land is left. (pp. 71–72)

With her considerable knowledge of American culinary rhythms over the last century, Shapiro (1986) has provided an historical context for the 1980s yuppie food excesses.

> Our contemporary food craze shares more than a blinkered culinary outlook with the craze of the last century. . . . In the late nineteenth century an expanding middle class was using food as a way to define itself, not only by imitating the dainty preferences of the rich, but by carefully avoiding the hallmarks of the poor. . . . The near-total concentration on upwardly mobile eating has also resulted in a near-total lack of social consciousness on the part of the new culinary movement. In striking distinction from the last century, today's food experts display little interest in the diet of the poor and hungry. Feeding the helpless is seen as a job for those with a professional interest in such things, not for lovers of fine cooking. (pp. 231–32)

4. In response to this nutritional truism, one food expert at Yale University has made several radical suggestions for changing the current financial bias toward unhealthful food: (1) use regulation and legislation to underwrite healthful foods, "so that carrots cost a quarter of what they cost now"; (2) tax unhealthful foods so that "if carrots cost a quarter of what they cost now, carrot cake would cost twice what it costs"; (3) ban food advertisements aimed at kids, or give equal time for public-service announcements that advertise nutritious fare; (4) help people become more active by using money generated from taxing unhealthful foods to build bike paths and enhance physical education in schools (Drexler, 1996, pp. 27–28). Though it is doubtful these suggestions would even pass legal challenges, the originator's ideas do provide provocative alternatives to the current corporate bias in favor of processed foods.

5. Belasco (1989) nicely illustrated class differences in attitudes regarding food reform in his description of a typical 1980s restaurant scene:

Thus at restaurants, while white-collar consumers ordered ascetic salads, blue-collar customers seeking immediate gratification filled up with foods that, however unhealthy, tasted good. Overindulging in the present was also a way of celebrating escape from past scarcity. While the middle class countercuisine venerated ethnic and folk foods that fit within the wider paradigm of "living lightly"—voluntary poverty-people with poor backgrounds were less willing to give up the culinary symbols of affluence: sugar . . . fats . . . highly refined white flour . . . and meat. While affluent people could afford more of these emblems, they took them more for granted and were perhaps more secure in cutting back voluntarily. (p. 198)

6. A good example of the anti-health dynamic was "the Cajun craze, for the food was clearly reactionary: rich in calories, fat, salt and, if blackened, carcinogens. It also embodied regressive, Reagan era values: enjoy today and damn the consequences" (Belasco, 1989, p. 237).

It has been my experience that vegetarians and others practicing even more restrictive eating behavior often are vulnerable to the anti-health dynamic since many self-described vegetarians (in terms of their actual eating behavior) singsong between vegetarianism and the junk food they consumed in their "impure" past. Eating on principle is fine when things are going your way; but a hot fudge sundae is called for when having "one of those days."

7. "For the ultimate in home cooking, why go out when you could just as easily stay in and tear open an envelope of dry onion soup mix," Belasco (1989) asked with a twinkle in his eye.

Heading back up the suburban driveway, they looked to mass culture itself as perhaps the last preserve of what they called "forthright food"—meat loaf and instant mashed potatoes, Jell-O mold, S'mores, Rice Krispies cookies, English muffin pizzas. Perhaps, as the camp/pop artists of the early 1960s had known, the best way to resist kitsch was to embrace it wholeheartedly. Like Andy Warhol . . . idolized Campbell's soup." (p. 238)

8. Always making connections between food and cultural behavior, Mintz (1996) has extrapolated that, "to the extent that this is a gender-marked phenomenon, anorexia and bulimia may come to look like no more than merely the flip side of the self-constructed beautiful You" (p. 7).

9. In an oppositional way, dieting also could be seen as anti-spiritual because close scrutiny of the foods we eat becomes the opposite of a spiritual discipline:

> Dieting is antispiritual because it focuses on a part of the created self at the expense of the whole. Counting calories (or whatever) focuses so narrowly on the size-obsessed "shoulds" of eating that it obscures our broader needs for acceptance, pleasure, nurture, and fulfillment. (Bringle, 1993, p. 61)

Learning to accept, care for, and love ourselves in our bodies must come before, not after, attempts to lose weight. In Bringle's words, "the supple soul is the one who joyously anticipates sitting down to the heavenly banquet—and who is able to do so with exuberant unconcern for whether or not the bread is buttered or the milk is 98 percent fat free" (p. 62).

10. Tisdale (1993) has illustrated this point with an account of her own dieting experience with Weight Watchers. She quotes founder Jean Nidetch who unempathically commented that "most fat people need to be hurt badly before they do something about themselves" (p. 65). Realizing that her dieting experience left her hating "the endlessness of it, the turning of food into portions and exchanges, everything measured out, permitted, denied. I hated the very idea of 'maintenance,' " Tisdale finally realized that she did not just hate the diet. She was sick of the way she acted on a diet: "The way I whined, my niggardly, penny-pitching behavior. What I liked in myself seemed to shrivel and disappear when I dieted. Slowly, slowly I saw these things. I saw that my pain was cut from whole cloth, imaginary, my own invention" (p. 65). In the end, Tisdale saw the real point of dieting was dieting: "I saw how much time I'd spent on something ephemeral, something that simply wasn't important, didn't matter. I saw that the real point of dieting is dieting—to not be done with it, ever" (p. 65).

CHAPTER SIX,
DISTURBED EATING, pp. 87–104

1. A student of mine intuited *Utne Reader's* 1993 cover story on "food guilt" by several years when she described women reminiscing about food in my 1988 "Food and Feminism" course oral histories. "Food is to these women as a Bible is to a spiritual person."

2. Shapiro (1986) has vividly described the 1950s scene when diets spread like wildfire with the birth of the dieting industry in America:

> All the passion and imagination that domestic scientists had devoted to taming the appetite was revived and magnified in the dieting industry. The techniques of cooking had been quietly disappearing on their own, as after-dinner mints teamed up successfully with grapefruit. Now, in place

of kitchen wisdom, an infinitude of detail about calorie counting, cottage cheese, and carrot sticks poured out of books and magazines, becoming the center of American culinary life. This gigantic social and commercial enterprise is still with us, and although men now diet chiefly for their health, women continue to diet in homage to a moral asceticism rooted centuries deep. (pp. 233–34)

3. In her lively account of her experience making a living as an aerobics instructor as she struggled to become a published feminist writer, Valdes (1995) described the 1990s gym scene from a moral perspective: "Women's fitness as we now know it truly is our newest patriarchal religion, based in principle as much on ritualized pain and suffering as any of the Judeo-Christian ones that came before it" (pp. 18–19). Valdes also has made the connection of guilt and shame as a by-product of patriarchy. It was a great relief for her "to finally recognize the female obsession with thinness and fitness as an extension of the hurt we suffer at the hands of a patriarchal society, a society that even convinces us to hurt ourselves, so that we are kept from the real business of our lives" (p. 19).

4. Chambers' observation coincides with a 1993 survey by *Essence* magazine that found 54 percent of black women to be at high risk for developing an eating disorder. "It's become a generational and class issue," says Audrey Chapman, a Howard University psychology professor. "Many middle-class blacks who are assimilated into the white culture— and teenagers too—want to be thin, thinner, thinnest" (Too fat?, 1996, p. 68).

5. Black students, for example, have referred me to a song, "Baby Got Back," celebrating the full-sized buttocks of some black women, when they argue that cultural press for thinness is greater for white than black women.

6. In my own clinical practice, I have found that approximately two-thirds of my clients who have eating issues also have experienced sexual abuse, often incest, prior to the onset of eating disturbances. This figure coincides with a 1993 Renfrew study that found 61 percent of its anorexic and bulimic patients had been sexually abused before the age of nineteen (Ross, 1996).

7. In my clinical work with women obsessed with fat, I repeatedly have been struck with the women's personal descriptions of fat as an alien intruder onto their own bodies; for example, referring to fat as an "it" ("getting it off; keeping it off") rather than as an integral part of their physical body ("wanting to lose weight; making myself smaller"). This linguistic

peculiarity perhaps reflects the view that fat is an "unnatural growth, akin to a cancerous tumor" (Seid, 1989, p. 22).

8. Each year as my students analyze local newspapers' messages about food in the weekly food section over a period of several months, they find that the food pages are consistent in their fat oppressive messages for women to reduce and minimize food intake, while also giving expression to the desire for special foods all humans seem to possess.

9. As expressed in the "zine" language of a young punk feminist:

> But really I'm fat. According to mainstream feminist theory, I don't even exist. I know that women do often look in the mirror and think that they are fatter than they are. And yes, this is a problem. But the analysis can't stop there. There are women who *are* fat, and that needs to be dealt with. Rather than just reassuring people, "No, you're not fat, you're just curvy," maybe we should be demystifying fat and dealing with fat politics as a whole. And I don't mean maybe, I mean it's a necessity. Once we realize that fat is not "inherently bad" (and I can't even believe I'm writing that—"inherently bad"—it sounds so ridiculous), then we can work out the problem as a whole instead of dealing only with this very minute part of it. All forms of oppression work together, and so they have to be fought together. (Lamm, 1995, p. 91)

The notion that fat oppression goes hand-in-hand with patriarchy should be thoughtfully considered. The author often has had female students and clients comment on their boyfriends'/husbands' use of fat references as a means of gaining control in the relationship. For example, the comment "when we go out tonight, why don't you leave the fat at home" is a powerful way to make the female partner feel inadequate and apologetic in her relationship with this man.

10. As one of the author's students expressed her view of the situation, "while feminism is attempting to *gain* power and *expand* opportunities for women, diet clinics all over the place are trying to *reduce* us."

CHAPTER SEVEN,
HEALING OURSELVES WITH FOOD, pp. 105–115

1. As one mother whose daughter nearly died as a result of her eating disorder expressed her objection to this sort of advertising, "models of the '90s who look like 12–year-old children and who are nicknamed Skeleton should not be the role models of our children" (Bass, 1994, p.16). Coca-Cola subsequently pulled the offending ads because of pressure from this group of irate mothers.

2. Unfortunately, the brand director's original decision was reversed by Omega's chairman; but the brand director subsequently wrote the publisher of *Vogue*, expressing his hope that the tremendous support and encouragement his company had received from the media and especially from the public would encourage the magazine's editorial staff to address these consuming issues in future advertising layouts.

3. The introduction to the Fall, 1996, fashion edition of *The New York Times Magazine* explained that influential newspaper's new fashion philosophy:

> If how we look is ultimately a function of how we see, then our capacity to appreciate ourselves and one another has been severely limited by our habit of comparing ourselves—however understandably—with actresses and models. In nearly every case, it is a losing proposition: we come off looking pretty good, at best, or (more often) not so good, or somehow not good enough. But experience, mercifully, provides us with another way of thinking about this business of appearances. . . . On the pages that follow, you'll meet women of all ages, from all walks of life. They look great. They look like themselves. They invite comparisons to no one. (How Do We Look?, 1996)

4. Food anthropologist Sidney Mintz has observed, "Being able to eat a great deal—the ability to do it—is one important way to say one is free and secure. The sense of being able to sit back with one's belly full and say, 'This is a good life, a great country' is very important in our history" (as cited in Drexler, 1996, p. 25).

5. Drexler (1996) has itemized the losses: "As a means to civilize children, teaching them that their identity and worth were bound up in how they related to other people—in cooking a meal together, passing the salt, noticing when a sibling was missing a fork, not leaving the table in the middle of dinner" (p. 24).

6. In support of Child as a positive role model, consider Christopher Lydon's accolade: "Julia Child reopened the American kitchen as an arena of Old World sensuality and delight. At the same time she contributed her own example . . . of a woman at home in the world, entirely herself" (1996, p. 11).

7. It is revealing that, after four years of the National Fluid Milk Processor Promotion Board (A.K.A. This National Dairy Council) pushing greater adult milk consumption via photos of well-known media stars with milk moustaches, this same group has capped their advertising campaign with a 1998 photo of Donna Shalala, Secretary of Health and Human Services, telling us in national news publications that Americans are not getting enough calcium, which could lead to osteoporosis. She suggests that the best way to load up on calcium is to drink lowfat or fat free milk. the ad copy concludes with Shalala's statement that a full thermos always is kept "in the cabinet." Talk about a fox in the chicken coop!

CHAPTER EIGHT, TRANSPOSING THE PERSONAL AND POLITICAL, pp. 117–132

1. The term "eating issues" in this discussion refers to thoughts, feelings, and behaviors in relation to food. It does not refer necessarily to particular body types or sizes. Obviously an anorexic woman will be extremely small in size; but bulimic women and compulsive eaters come in all sizes and shapes.

2. This question was intellectually considered by an Appetite for Change group as "homework" one week. Each member of this group had previous experience with dieting centers before entering Appetite for Change. Members' answers to the question, "Is Appetite for Change different from weight reduction programs such as Weight Watchers, etc?" were discussed over dinner the following week, and could be summarized as follows:

> **a.** The goal of Appetite for Change is not to lose weight. No one will be punished or have positive reinforcement withheld because of failure to either lose weight or accomplish other behavioral expectations of those running the group. One woman described the mood in Appetite for Change as one where "we cannot fail here." Weight Watchers, for example, has been known to award pins and other tangibles to members who reach certain goals pertaining to their weight. Other times important weight losses are announced during the diet center meeting though actual weighing-in is done in private. The women did acknowledge that Weight Watchers and its clones do work on a positive reinforcement model. But as group members pointed out, cultural pressure against being "fat" is very much in evidence in dieting centers and, therefore, is enough of a negative reinforcer to influence women's behavior.

> **b.** A major goal of Appetite for Change, on the other hand, is to examine and challenge assumptions underlying our culture's attitudes toward food and body size. No goals are imposed on any woman by other individuals in the group or the therapist. The goals each woman sets for herself upon entering the group are respected by the therapist and other group members. However, most group members modify their personal goals for the group experience over time. Learning of the cultural manipulation of body size, for example, usually results in a woman developing a more healthy resistance to social pressures for her to become smaller than she is at the present time. If a woman were to apply for membership in Appetite for Change only to "help her lose weight," the therapist would

counsel her about the pitfalls involved in such an approach, and offer alternative ways to possibly change one's eating behavior. The woman then would be free to create other individual goals for membership in the group or to look elsewhere for a weight reduction program if that still remained her primary reason for seeking group membership.

c. Appetite for Change is not a behavioral modification system in the rigid sense of large dieting centers. Group members "think as free individuals about the intellectual and spiritual components of our eating issues" as one group member clarified the difference between Appetite for Change and traditional dieting groups.

d. As mentioned above, Appetite for Change is based on feminist principles where "we use this analysis to allow us to stand outside the cultural press regarding food," as one woman described the process. From this "view from the margin," women can delve into underlying issues, ones beneath the food issues, to see how and why they express other emotional issues through the medium of food. Another woman concurred with this analysis that "food is the touchstone allowing for the expression of so many other issues."

e. Finally it was observed by one member that "women must integrate their cooking and eating experiences in Appetite for Change with their eating behavior during the rest of the week." A quick "check in" at the beginning of each week's group is intended to address each woman's ability to utilize the previous week's experience in group when making her food decisions in the days following that group meeting. (These points are a summary of responses to a personal correspondence from the editorial board of *Women and Therapy*, Jan. 26, 1992.)

3. Many women struggling with food in weight reduction programs or on individual diets talk of food simply as "fuel" for the body. They often use the machine model, that maintaining a certain weight simply involves the understanding that you take in so many calories via food and expend so many calories via physical exercise. They see their food issues simply as a mechanistic problem of the body. Prior to joining Appetite for Change, most group members have had impressive amounts of experience with weight reduction programs and diets that encourage this machine model.

4. A majority of Americans probably fit Mintz's (1996) profile:

Eating out frequently, often choosing fast foods, as well as ordering takeout food to eat at home; eating much prepared and packaged foods, which require only intense heat or nothing at all to be "cooked"; continuing to eat diets high in animal protein, salt, fats, and processed sugars, low in fresh fruits and vegetables; drinking more soda than tap water; and consuming substantial quantities of labeled (low fat no cholesterol fat free lots of fiber no palm oil good for you) foods, packaged to encourage the consumer to feel less guilty about what he is really choosing to eat. (pp. 117–18)

5. Jenkins (1992) has spoken eloquently and often on this theme: "Food matters—and not just because we all have to eat two or three meals a day. It matters because it is a profound and important way of connecting our-selves with the earth, with our history, with our communities and with each other, of guaranteeing our health as individuals and as social ani-mals, as well as the health of the world we live in" (p. 17).

6. Pimental has been grimly quoted as follows:

> As the Earth's population grows geometrically . . . pressure will be placed on arable land, water, energy, and the resources needed to keep up the food supply. Over the next 60 years, if current growth trends continue, the US population will double. Grains will probably be used not for animal feed but directly to feed 520 million people. (Drexler, 1996, p. 29)

7. Jenkins (1992) also has described an unappetizing scenario for the meat supply consumed by Americans:

> Feed-lot beef, fattened on grain that could and should be put to more effi-cient uses, hogs and poultry raised on antibiotics and other drugs to make them grow fatter faster, veal calves that because of their deliberately weak-ened condition must be constantly medicated to keep them alive for slaughter, are all indications of tremendous waste, as well as of the threat to human health from the residues of such additives in our meat. (p. 18)

8. "Voting with your fork" is the axiom of a group Jenkins directed for many years, Oldways Preservation and Exchange Trust, a Boston-based nonprofit organization that seeks to educate people about traditional ways of handling food.

CONCLUSIONS, pp. 133–136

1. Demographers have coined the phrase "the pig in the python" in refer-ence to the population bulge created by the bumper crop of babies born in America after soldiers returned from World War II. This age cohort, birth years 1949–1965, became the 1980s yuppies, known for their affluent ma-terialistic excesses. The oldest baby-boomers (as they were re-named in the 1990s) began turning fifty in 1995. Because they comprise the largest segment of the American population at the turn of the twenty-first cen-tury, the so-called pig possesses great potential for influencing public pol-icy, in addition to cultural style, for the remaining decades of their collective life.

2. A national environmental magazine (Rauber, 1997) reported on what could serve as a prototype for public education's potential contribution to school children's growing awareness of the impact of individual food choices on one's own health and the health of the planet. The Edible Schoolyard in Berkeley, California, is the brain-child of Alice Waters, founder of the famed Chez Panisse restaurant and "apostle of organic produce and seasonal cooking" (p. 24), and represents a collaboration of public and private interests to improve children's diets while also providing them with lifelong tools for maintaining a healthy interaction with the world around them. The school children transformed a vacant lot into the Edible Schoolyard where they grow vegetables, herbs, and flowers for use in school lunches that also are prepared by the students. Appreciation for global food resources grows out of these hands-on endeavors: "What the Edible Schoolyard shows is that learning doesn't have to stop at lunchtime; kids can take care of the earth and themselves, and have fun doing it" (p. 25).

3. In her writing, hooks (1982) originally created this concept as part of her analysis of the intersections of race and gender in America. However, hooks (1984; 1989) subsequently expanded the notion of "Other" in her consideration of class divisions among women within the United States and between American women and the vast majority of women around the globe. hooks (1994) is quite aware of the irony that American (a.k.a. white) feminism has been vigilant with regard to male dominance, and yet remains insensitive to the treatment of the world's subsistence farmers, the vast majority of whom are women.

Bibliography

Bascom, W. (1969). *The Yoruba of southwestern Nigeria*. New York: Holt, Rinehart and Winston, Inc.

Bass, A. (1994, April 25). "Anorexic marketing" faces boycott. *The Boston Globe*, p. 16.

Belasco, W. (1989). *Appetite for change: How the counterculture took on the food industry, 1966–1988*. New York: Pantheon.

Boserup, E. (1970). *Women's role in economic development*. London: Gallen and Unwin.

Bringle, M. L. (1993, November/December). Is eating the oldest sin? *Utne Reader, 60*, 61–62.

Brown, C., & Jasper, K. (1993). Why weight? why women? why now? In C. Brown & K. Jasper (Eds.), *Consuming passions: Feminist approaches to weight preoccupation and eating disorders*. (pp. 16–35). Toronto: Second Story Press.

Brown, J. K. (1970). A note on the division of labor by sex. *American Anthropologist. 72*, 1073–1078.

Brown, L. S., & Rothblum, E. D. (Eds.). (1989). *Fat oppression and psychotherapy: A feminist perspective*. New York: Haworth Press.

Brumberg, J. J. (1988). *Fasting girls: The history of anorexia nervosa*. New York: Penguin Books.

Brumberg, J. J. (1990, April 9). Feed your head. *The Nation*, pp. 494–496.

Carpenter, C. R. (1942). Characteristics of social behavior in non-human primates. *Transactions of the New York Academy of Sciences, 2*(4), 248–258.

Chambers, V. (1995). Betrayal feminism. In B. Findlen (Ed.), *Listen Listen up: Voices from the next feminist generation* (pp. 21–28). Seattle: Seal Press.

Chernik, A. B. (1995). The body politic. In B. Findlen (Ed.), *Listen up: Voices from the next feminist generation* (pp. 75–84). Seattle: Seal Press.

Chernin, K. (1981). *The obsession: Reflections on the tyranny of slenderness.* New York: Harper and Row.

Chernin, K. (1985). *The hungry self: Women, eating and identity.* New York: Harper and Row.

Clarke, K. (1993, November/December). Growing hunger. *Utne Reader, 60,* 63–68.

Clinton signs bill limiting residues in foods. (1996, August 4). *The Boston Globe,* p. A30.

Cobb, N. (1994, September 21). The mall meal plan. *The Boston Globe,* pp. 73, 76.

Colbin, A. (1986). *Food and healing.* New York: Ballantine Books.

Colborn, T., Dumanoski, D. & Myers, J. P. (1997). *Our stolen future: Are we threatening our fertility, intelligence, and survival?* New York: Dutton.

Daley, B. (1994, March 27). Students learn to design menus. *The Boston Globe,* p. E4.

Davison, J. (1996). *Voices from Mutira.* London: Lynne Rienner Publishers.

Draper, P. (1975). !Kung women: Contrasts in sexual egalitarianism in foraging and sedentary contexts. In R. R. Reiter (Ed.), *Toward an anthropology of women* (pp. 77–109). New York: Monthly Review Press.

Drexler, M. (1996, July 21). Ten reasons why it's so hard to change our eating habits. *The Boston Globe,* pp. 16–27.

Ehrenreich, B. (1989). *Fear of falling: The inner life of the middle class.* New York: Pantheon Books.

Enloe, C. (1989). *Bananas, beaches and bases: Making feminist sense of international politics.* Berkeley: University of California Press.

Estioko-Griffin, A. A., & Griffin, P. B. (1975). Woman the hunter: The Agta. In R. R. Reiter (Ed.), *Toward an anthropology of women* (pp. 121–151). New York: Monthly Review Press.

Faragher, J. M. (1991). The Midwestern farming family, 1850. In L. K. Kerber & J. S. DeHart (Eds.), *Women's America* (pp. 119–132). New York: Oxford University Press.

Farb, P. F., & Armelagos, G. (1980). *Consuming passions: The anthropology of eating.* New York: Washington Square Press.

Fink, D. (1986). *Open country, Iowa: rural women, tradition and change.* Buffalo: State University of New York Press.

Foreman, J. (1995, October 30). Fat liability. *The Boston Globe,* p. A22.

Fox, B. (Ed.). (1980). *Hidden in the household: Women's domestic labour under capitalism.* Toronto: The Women's Press.

Friedl, E. (1975). *Women and men.* New York: Holt, Rinehart and Winston.

Friedl, E. (1978). Society and sex roles. *Human Nature*, 1(4), 68–75.

GB. (1987, February). Food for thought. *Heresies*, 3.

Goodall, J. (1968). The behavior of free-living chimpanzees in the Gombe Stream Reserve. *Animal Behavior Monographs*, *1*, 165–311.

Goodall, J. (1973). Cultural elements in a chimpanzee community. In E. W. Menzel (Ed.), *Precultural primate behavior* (pp. 3–30). New York: Alan R. Liss, Inc.

Goodman, E. (1998, April 16). A food fight over the meaning of organic farming. *The Boston Globe*, p. A27.

Gordon, K. D. (1987). Evolutionary perspectives on human diet. In F. Johnston (Ed.), *Nutritional Anthropology* (pp. 144–184). Basel, Switzerland: Karger.

Hardeman, N. (1981). *Shucks, shocks, and hominy blacks: Corn as a way of life in pioneer America*. Baton Rouge: Louisiana State University Press.

Harris, M. (1975). *Culture, people, nature*. New York: Thomas Y. Crowell.

hooks, b. (1982). *Black looks: Race and representation*. Boston: South End Press.

hooks, b. (1984). *Feminist theory: From margin to center*. Boston: South End Press.

hooks, b. (1989). *Talking back: Thinking feminist, thinking black*. Boston: South End Press.

hooks, b. (1994). *Outlaw culture: Resisting representations*. New York: Routledge.

How do we look? (1996, August 25). *The New York Times Magazine*, 81.

Iggers, J. (1993, November/December). Innocence lost: Our complicated relationship with food. *Utne Reader*, *60*, 56–60.

Jenkins, N. H. (1992). Voting with your fork. *The Boston Globe*, pp. 17–19.

Jensen, J. (1996). With these hands: Women on the Lord. In C. Sachs (Ed.), *Gendered fields*. Boulder, CO: Westview Press.

Julian, S. (1997, September 24). Moving toward a healthier plate. *The Boston Globe*, pp. E2, E5, E6.

Kagan, D. (1990, December 3). Add health to haute and stir. *Insight*, 8–17.

Kaptchuk, T. (1982, November). The holistic logic of Chinese medicine. *Science Digest*, 32–35.

Kennedy, D. (1998, February 13). Meat puppets. *The Boston Phoenix*, pp. 4–7.

Lamm, N. (1995). It's a big fat revolution. In B. Findlen (Ed.), *Listen up: Voices from the next feminist generation*. Seattle: Seal Press.

Landtman, G. (1927). *The Kiwai Papuans of British New Guinea*. London: Macmillan.

Lappe, F. M. (1971). *Diet for a small planet*. New York: Ballantine.

Lappe, F. M., & Collins, J. (1977). *Food first: Beyond the myth of scarcity*. New York: Ballantine.

Lee, R. B. (1979). *The !Kung San: Men, women and work in a foraging society.* New York: Cambridge University Press.

Lee, R. B., & deVore, I. (1968). *Man the hunter.* Chicago: Aldine.

Lenski, G. & Lenski, J. (1978). *Human societies.* New York: McGraw-Hill.

Levenstein, H. (1988). *Revolution at the table: The transformation of the American diet.* New York: Oxford University Press.

Lindner, L. (1991, April 28). Dieting: It isn't kid stuff. *The Boston Globe, The Good Health Magazine,* 18, 20.

Liss-Levinson, N. (1988). Disorders of desire: women, sex, and food. *Women and Therapy,* 7, 121–129.

Lydon, C. (1996, March 27–April 9). The feminist we'll remember. *The Improper Bostonian,* 11–16.

Martin, M. K. & Voorhies, B. (1975). *Female of the species.* New York: Columbia University Press.

McGrew, W. C. (1981). The female chimpanzee as evolutionary prototype. In F. Dahlberg (Ed.), *Woman the gatherer* (pp. 35–73). New Haven: Yale University Press.

McLaughlin, P. (1996, January 15). What if nobody's fat? *Cape Cod Times,* pp. C1–C2.

McPhee, M. (1996, June 8). Thin may be in, but it's no answer. *The Boston Globe,* p. A20.

Meloy, E. (1993, November/December). Carp seviche and jerked squirrel. *Utne Reader,* 60, 69–73.

Merchant, C. (1989). *Ecological revolutions: Nature, gender and science in New England.* Chapel Hill: University of North Carolina Press.

Miles, R. (1988). *The woman's history of the world.* New York: Harper and Row.

Miller, S. (1979). *Food for thought: A new look at food and behavior.* Englewood Cliffs, NJ: Prentice Hall.

Mintz, S. W. (1996). *Tasting food, tasting freedom.* Boston: Beacon Press.

Morgan, L. (1962). *League of the Iroquois.* New York: Corinth Books.

O'Kelly, C. G. (1980). *Women and men in society.* New York: D. van Nostrand.

O'Neill, M. (1996a, March 10). The morality of fat in low-fat theology. *The New York Times Magazine,* 37–39.

O'Neill, M. (1996b, September 1). A pinch of common sense. *The New York Times Magazine,* 51–52.

O'Neill, M. (1998, January 4). Bay watch. *The New York Times Magazine,* 47–48.

Orbach, S. (1978). *Fat is a feminist issue.* New York: Paddington.

Perrin, G. (1991, August 21). Losing it. *The Boston Globe,* pp. 77, 82.

Pollan, M. (1994, March 24). The seed conspiracy. *The New York Times Magazine,* 49–50.

Pringle, H. (1998, April). New women of the Ice Age. *Discover,* 19, 62–69.

Rauber, P. (1997, November/December). The edible schoolyard. *Sierra, 82*(6), 24–25.

Reichl, R. (1995, April 2). You might as well say "bon appetit." *The New York Times*, Education Life section, pp. 18, 19.

Richards, A. (1939). *Land, labour and diet in Northern Rhodesia: An economic sudy of the Bemba tribe*. London: Oxford University Press.

Robb, C. (1989, April 21). Diet programs spotlight health. *The Boston Globe*, pp. 37, 42.

Ross, J. (1996, June). Hunger pains. *Allure*, 132, 134, 136.

Roth, G. (1982). *Feeding the hungry heart*. New York: Signet.

Roth, G. (1984). *Breaking free from compulsive eating*. New York: Signet.

Roth, G. (1991). *When food is love*. New York: Plume.

Sachs, C. (1996). *Gendered fields*. Boulder, CO: Westview Press.

Sahlins, M. (1972). *Stone age economics*. New York: Aldine-Atherton.

Seid, R. P. (1989). *Never too thin: Why women are at war with their bodies*. New York: Prentice Hall Press.

Shapiro, L. (1986). *Perfection salad: women and cooking at the turn of the century*. New York: Farrar, Straus & Giroux.

Shorter, E. (1976). Women's work: What difference did capitalism make? *Theory and Society. 3*, 514.

Shostack, M. (1981). *Nisa*. New York: Vintage.

Shroff, F. M. (1993). Deliciosa! the body, passion, and pleasure. In C. Brown and K. Jasper (Eds.), *Consuming passions: Feminist approaches to weight preoccupation and eating disorders*. (pp. 109–117). Toronto: Second Story Press.

Silber, T. (1986). Anorexia nervosa in blacks and hispanics. *International Journal of Eating Disorders, 5*, 121–128.

Slocum, S. (1975). Woman the gatherer: male bias in anthropology. In R. R. Reiter (Ed.), *Toward an anthropology of women* (pp. 36–50). New York: Monthly Review Press.

Sojourner. (1994). Editorial, p. 3.

Stewart, C. (1996, September 7/8). Fatso versus skinny. *The Patriot Ledger*, p. 20.

Strathern, M. (1992). *Women in between*. New York: Seminar Press.

Stratton, J. L. (1981). *Pioneer women: Voices from the Kansas frontier*. New York: Simon & Schuster.

Thompson, B. W. (1992). "A way outa no way": Eating problems among African-American, latina, and white women. *Gender and Society, 6*(4), 546–561.

Thompson, B. W. (1994). *A hunger so wide and so deep*. Minneapolis: University of Minnesota Press.

Tilly, L. A., & Scott, J. W. (1987). *Women, work and family*. New York: Routledge.

Tisdale, S. (1993, November/December). A diet of denial. *Utne Reader, 60*, 64–65.

Too fat? Too thin? (1996, June 3). *People*, 64–74.

Ulrich, L. T. (1991). The ways of her household. In L. K. Kerber & J. S. De-Hart (Eds.), *Women's America* (pp. 41–51). New York: Oxford University Press.

Valdes, A. L. (1995). Ruminations of a feminist aerobics instructor. In B. Findlen (Ed.), *Listen up: Voices from the next feminist generation*. Seattle: Seal Press.

Wajcman, J. (1991). *Feminism confronts technology*. Cambridge, UK: Polity Press.

Wells, T., & Sim, F. G. (1987). *Till they have faces: women as consumers*. Penang, Malaysia: Isis International.

Wertheimer, B. M. (1977). *We were there: The story of working women in America*. New York: Pantheon Books.

Yamada, K. (1995, April 7). Toward leaner meat and celery sticks without strings. *The Wall Street Journal*, p. B1.

Zihlman, A. (1981). Women as shapers of human adaptation. In F. Dahlberg (Ed.), *Woman the gatherer*. New Haven: Yale University Press.

Index

About the Author

CATHERINE MANTON, Ph.D., a clinical psychologist, is Associate Professor of Women's Studies at the University of Massachusetts at Boston, where, for the last decade, she has taught the course "Food and Feminism." Professor Manton's articles have appeared in various academic journals including *Trotter Institute Review* and *Women and Therapy.* She also incorporates culinary healing into her private clinical practice, and enjoys cooking for friends in her large kitchen and tending her edible garden.

ISBN 0-89789-448-0